Let's Develop!

"To live life without joy, day after day, year after year, is as deadening to the human spirit as it is to live without having enough food to eat or a roof over your head," says Dr. Fred Newman. Yet that's how millions of us are living our lives — going through the motions, feeling trapped.

Let Dr. Newman show you how to turn your life into a play that *you* direct! Don't just change your behavior…create a whole new life!

Let's Develop! will help *you*:

- ❖ practice giving instead of "getting." It's better for your emotional health!

- ❖ stop trying to find "solutions" to your "problems." Live your life instead!

- ❖ break out of the roles you're stuck in with your family and your friends. Be creative!

- ❖ meet new people. Yes, do talk to strangers!

- ❖ see how there's no such thing as "addiction" — to alcohol, drugs, food or anything else. You *can* make a choice!

- ❖ make sex more fun. Try friendosexuality!

- ❖ take advantage of the "pointlessness" of life. Have an adventure!

- ❖ make decisions without knowing what the outcome will be. You never know!

- ❖ stop obsessing about how you look. Change who you are!

- ❖ deal with severe illness, chronic pain and getting older. Use them to grow!

Let's Develop!

A Guide to Continuous Personal Growth

Dr. Fred Newman
with Dr. Phyllis Goldberg

COMMUNITY LITERACY RESEARCH PROJECT • NEW YORK

The people who appear in this book are fictional
characters based on composites of actual patients in
Dr. Fred Newman's therapy practice.

Community Literacy Research Project, Inc.
500 Greenwich Street, Suite 201
New York, New York 10013

© 1994 by Fred Newman

Library of Congress Catalog Number: 94-68612

Newman, Fred
Let's Develop! A Guide to Continuous Personal Growth

ISBN 0-9628621-6-9

TYPOGRAPHY BY ILENE ADVERTISING, NEW YORK
BOOK AND COVER DESIGN BY DAVID NACKMAN

01   00   99   98   97   96   95   94   5   4   3   2

Manufactured in the United States of America

Contents

Acknowledgments

I am tremendously fortunate in having as my publishers Gabrielle Kurlander and Candice Sherman, two brilliantly creative business-women — both beautiful in every way — who thought enough of this book to develop it beyond my capability. I am even more fortunate in having them as friends who care so deeply for me and my work.

It is a pleasure to acknowledge their marvelous and hardworking staff at Castillo International: David Nackman, the very talented graphic artist who designed the book; Margo Grant, Jessica Massad, Chris Street and Kim Svoboda, the dedicated production team which more than shares my commitment to putting practice first and painstakingly saw the manuscript through its many stages; Diane Stiles, my good friend the production manager, who lovingly assumed responsibility for making it all happen, and right on time; Ilene Hinden, the publishers' versatile assistant; Donna Kaseta, Roger Grunwald, Lisa Linnen and the rest of the enthusiastic sales staff; and Omar Ali, Pat Wictor and Chuck Knapp, of the famous shipping team.

Dr. Lois Holzman, the distinguished developmental psychologist who has been my chief collaborator over the last 15 years in articulating a theory of social development and putting it into practice pedagogically at the Barbara Taylor School in Harlem, New York and at the Manhattan campus of Empire State Col-

lege, read the manuscript and gave me excellent advice. Jackie
Salit, my wonderful friend and political colleague, also read the
manuscript and thought it "correct." I am deeply grateful to both
of them.

Along with the thousands of people who have been patients in
social therapy over the last 25 years, the staffs of the East Side
Center for Social Therapy and the East Side Institute for Short
Term Psychotherapy — Mark Balsam, Bette Braun, Esther Farmer,
Kathy Fiess, Rena Filipanics, Mary Fridley, Dr. Lenora Fulani,
Nancy Green, Chris Helm, Nancy Henschel, Vera Hill, Dr. Lois
Holzman, Christine LaCerva, Gwen Lowenheim, Debra Pearl, Dr.
Hugh Polk, Freda Rosen, Carrie Sackett, Cathy Salit, Nancy
Salsarulo, Barbara Silverman, Karen Steinberg, Lorraine Stevens,
Gloria Strickland, Barbara Taylor, Ivonne Vazquez and Linda
Young — along with Murray Dabby, the director of the Atlanta
Center for Social Therapy, Joyce Dattner, the director of the West
Coast Center for Social Therapy in San Francisco, Helen Abel of
the West Coast Center, Evelyn Dougherty, the director of the
Boston Center for Social Therapy, and Elizabeth Hechtman, the
director of the Philadelphia Center for Social Therapy, are partners
in the necessary and presumptuous enterprise of creating a new
psychology. Cindy Little is yet another partner in that enterprise.

I am a philosopher by training. In the foolishly much-divided
world of academia, this means I am disqualified as a psychologist.
As a renegade who left philosophy, I am also persona non grata in
Plato's cave. I am, happily, a teacher without a department — not
to mention a university! Thanks, then, to the psychologists, phil-
osophers and activists in this country and around the world who
have taken our work seriously: Chris Aanstoos, Alexander
Adamsky, Gordon Baker, Paul Baker, David Bearison, Benjamin
Beit-Hallahmi, Guillermo Blanck, Erica Burman, Harry Daniels,
Dan Greenberg, Paolo Henry, Stanley Krippner, Jose Linaza,
Alfonso Luque, Ignacio Montero, John Morss, Ian Parker, Dan

Powell, Alberto Rosa, Miguel Serrano, Eleine Shepel, John Shotter and Paul Stenner.

Warren Seigel, the author of the foreword to this book, and Susan Massad, who wrote the "blurb" on the back, are both physicians of an unusual kind. They too believe in the Hippocratic dictum to "first do no harm." But they go much further, giving their intelligence and their compassion with utmost generosity. I am grateful to them for their thoughtful words, and honored to be their colleague and their friend.

Phyllis Goldberg, my "with," is everywhere in this book. She warmly and graciously and brilliantly made me examine my own "metaphysical mist" and gently yet ruthlessly insisted that I make philosophy and psychology as accessible to our readers as possible. She can rightfully take credit for as much or as little of the product as she wishes. The male ego that remains, however, is all mine.

Foreword

I am honored to have been asked to write the foreword for this book. By way of introduction, let me first tell you a few things about Dr. Fred Newman.

Dr. Newman is the most committed, enthusiastic and dedicated human being that I have ever met. Although many people are enthusiastic about their jobs, dedicated to their families, and committed to the positions they hold in society, Dr. Newman is enthusiastic about, dedicated and committed to — change! He consistently and tirelessly works for the improvement of the lives of human beings. He has labored for more than two decades to create something new — to create an environment in which people do not accept their "fate" in life, but instead, become active changers.

Dr. Newman is referred to by many as a "revolutionary." By his own admission, Dr. Newman strives for a total restructuring of the way people relate to each other and to the world. I tend to think of Dr. Newman not as a revolutionary, but as a visionary. He sees people (and the world) not as they are, but as they can be! He treats every person as a "producer" — a producer of change, someone who can make a difference in the world. To him, a human being is not merely a recipient of life, but someone who can actively *create* his or her life.

Dr. Newman is one of the rare people in our society who

refuses to accept the statement, "Oh, I (or we) can't do that!" He actively participates in reorganizing an environment that supports people to begin to say, "Yes, I *want* to do that!" He steadfastly believes that the human condition can change, because humans can change conditions!

❖

I was first introduced to Dr. Newman's social therapy in 1987. I was completing my residency in Pediatrics at a hospital in New York when social therapists Debra Pearl, Barbara Silverman and Dr. Hugh Polk came to the hospital to lecture.

The talk, "Depression in Children and Adolescents," was certainly enlightening! These therapists did not recite statistics on how many children and adolescents were depressed, had attempted suicide, had successfully committed suicide, etc. Instead, the message of their talk was how labeling patients as "depressed" kept them from getting better! Their talk was well received by the audience, but I was particularly struck by the speakers. There was something different about the way they talked about people — something new, something refreshing, something respectful.

I had spent the previous three years of my training in Pediatrics learning about the physical, emotional and psychological patterns of growth in children and adolescents, and these social therapists said something that had a profound effect on me. They proposed that the developmental process had no end. They said that although development often stopped, it could be reinitiated at any point in life. Even adults could grow and develop! This was certainly a radical concept.

A few months later, I attended a weekend retreat sponsored by the East Side Center for Social Therapy. The topic for the weekend was "Burnout in the Health Care Professions." As the Chief Resident for the Department of Pediatrics in an urban hospital, the topic seemed very appropriate for me, and I signed up. Once again, I was struck by the caring, dedicated and committed quality of the people I met, so different from so many of the "helping professionals" with whom I worked on a daily basis. Much of the discussion that weekend dealt with the difficulties involved in "not knowing." For example, when a person comes to my office with a physical complaint, I, as a doctor, am expected to "know" how to cure him or her. One person, even a medical doctor, cannot know everything, and this seems acceptable in our society. However, when a doctor does not "know" an answer, he or she is still expected to "know" what to do, e.g., refer the patient to a specialist, order tests, do additional reading.

The concept of being a "knower" in society has always left me frustrated. I have gone through many long and grueling years of traditional education — high school, college and medical school — but I have never felt like a "knower." I have never felt that I have all the answers. This has left me vulnerable to feeling like a fraud when I have attempted to be a "knower," and likewise, left me vulnerable to criticism when I have admitted to not "knowing."

Generally, our society does not value people who are not "knowers." In fact, huge institutions are devoted to knowledge and the imparting of this knowledge to others — usually called "students." The struggle around "knowledge" that I have gone through as I learned to do social therapy has been difficult, but relieving. Dr. Newman and his colleagues have taken me away from the paradigm that says "I must know everything!" and freed me to begin working openly with others, including my patients.

During my training in Adolescent Medicine (a subspecialty of Pediatrics), I became fascinated with the impact that emotionality (the mind) has on the physical (the body). So I entered a training program in social therapy run by Dr. Newman in September 1987.

At the time, I was becoming increasingly frustrated with mainstream traditional medicine. It is an institution which fosters the notion that the patient is merely the passive recipient of the doctor's "cure," and that disease can be conquered if only the patient strictly adheres to a particular diet, drug regimen or prescribed exercises. I believed it to be an institution that had become alienated from the people we served, and it was clear to me that something "radical" was necessary!

In my current position as the Director of Adolescent Medicine at several hospitals in New York, I am able to use my training in social therapy, and my experience with Dr. Newman and his colleagues, to help a community of adolescents that has, by and large, become alienated from the medical community. In setting up adolescent health care programs, I have used the social therapeutic model to help empower adolescents to "own" the program, and to take an active role in their own "cure." That is, they take part in determining what care they are given, and how and when they receive it. The program is for them, and it is produced by them.

❖

As is true for many people born in Brooklyn in the late 1950s, my family made the exodus to Long Island; they searched for a "better way of life" and "better education." And like most of my generation growing up in middle class white suburbia, I did have a good life and a good education. My parents, working class people, struggled to become middle class and to offer their children all of the things that they, growing up in Brooklyn, hadn't had. They paid a price for this upward mobility, but so did we!

My family was quite liberal, so I was exposed to many ideas about the world; ideas about how to relate to people who were "other" than me, and about respecting them in spite of our differences. And yet even with this liberal background, I really had no frame of reference. I had never really known anyone who was Black or Latino. Gays and lesbians were unknown in our community and working class people (although they certainly existed) were struggling to fit into the middle class.

When I became a doctor, I found myself working with inner-city people; suddenly I was relating to people of color from all over the world, with various histories, languages, and backgrounds. I certainly had my emotional reactions and struggles. But who could I talk to about these issues?

It was not until I came into social therapy that I found people who were in a position to teach me — about racism, classism, anti-Semitism, homophobia and sexism. These were people who would not only teach me about these issues in the world, but who would help me with these issues in my life.

As a student, and later as a patient with Dr. Newman, I came to learn how much the social institutions of racism, classism, sexism, homophobia and anti-Semitism have affected my life. But this "knowledge" wasn't the point. Through hard work with Dr. Newman and my therapy group, I have come to be able to go beyond the statements, "The world is racist" or "The world is homophobic." I have learned to help create the conditions where these institutions are not perpetuated. I have learned to take a stand *against* these institutions, and have become empowered enough to try to change them. That, I could only have learned from social therapy, and more specifically, from Dr. Newman.

One may wonder what Dr. Newman — a working class white Jewish man from the Bronx — knows (let alone could teach) about racism, homophobia, or sexism. But he has fought for the better part of his adult life against the very institutions that keep people down. He has taught me and others that it is possible to build and to create even though these "isms" exist, and he has shown us that we can be active changers of our lives and our society.

❖

It is for all of these reasons that I have come to love, admire, and respect Dr. Newman and the people — both therapists and patients — in social therapy. Dr. Newman does not merely work to "see" what exists; he actively works to create something better. He does not insist that he "knows" what needs to be done. Rather, he works to create an environment in which we — human beings — grow and develop, so that we can make the changes that *we* feel need to happen.

Let's Develop! is "must" reading for anyone who has ever wondered if his or her life could change. And it is "must" reading for "helping professionals" who truly want to help. Social therapy is an approach that has already touched thousands of lives, both in the United States and abroad. It's an approach that *can* lead to change — and to development!

— Warren M. Seigel, M.D.
New York City
July 1994

Introduction

In a year or so, I'll be 60. In our culture, that's an age when people start to think that you've acquired something called "wisdom." Don't make that mistake with me! I say that not to be self-degrading, or out of any sense of false modesty, but simply because I don't believe in wisdom (and surely not that you could get it just by getting older — our world is filled with aged dummies). What I do believe in is creative work — the everyday, unglamorous activity of ordinary people working together to create something that's needed or wanted by them, or that they simply choose to do. That's what I mean by development.

Let's Develop! is therefore not intended, and I sincerely hope it will not be used, as an Authoritative Source. It's more of a workbook, an exercise book. What I think we can use as we head into the uncharted social and emotional waters of the 21st century is practical help and support to create our own lives. That's what this book tries to give you.

I think *Let's Develop!,* like the social therapeutic approach expressed in it, ultimately has to do with the development of an attitude toward life — indeed, a developmental attitude toward life. As such, it is filled neither with definitions nor with endless advice. Rather, it is a book containing stories of people's lives and responses to those stories which, I hope, will help you to practice your own life more as an ongoing exercise in growth than as a set of roles to be routinely played out. We are all performers — among other things — and it enhances life immeasurably, in my opinion, to live it as an improvisational play that we and those close to us continuously create.

The practical question, from the social therapeutic point of view, is not *How much can I get from this?* Nor is it *What's the right thing to do?* Rather, in any and all life situations, good and bad, early and late, big and little, I urge that the question be *How do we develop from this?* That, as I see it, is an emotionally healthy attitude in a sometimes very sick world.

While the social and political ferment of the 1960s has had an obvious and, I believe, positive effect on my life, I don't feel any need or inclination to romanticize that particular moment of our collective and my personal history. Indeed, I have come to see that that era of liberal radicalism, when the words "Black liberation," "women's liberation" and "gay liberation" first entered the American vocabulary, was every bit as dogmatic and narrow as the more conservative '50s and '80s. Certainly, the '60s did not succeed in liberating the many millions of people who live in a more or less steady state of sometimes profound emotional pain.

In the 25 years during which I have been a therapist, I have learned that emotional pain is endemic in our postmodern, postindustrial society, in the same way that certain parasitic diseases are endemic in many tropical countries. Some people have acute cases and are likely to die, while many other people don't feel well and, from time to time, are incapacitated. Just about everyone has it. Given that reality, I have spent much of my energy during the last two decades of my life trying to answer two questions: Why is emotional pain so widespread? And does it have to be?

Now when I talk about trying to answer these questions, I don't mean trying to come up with a theory, "on paper." I mean doing something, in a very practical way, about people's emotional pain to change it.

While I was in high school, and for the six months that I attended college before joining the Army, I had a job in a grimy machine shop in the East 90s in Manhattan (the section of New York City that used to be known as Yorkville) where my older brother Maudie worked as a tool and die maker. It was here, watching him work, that I learned the distinction between the ready-made tools you buy in the hardware store (hammers, screwdrivers, saws) and the very sophisticated, one-of-a-kind, specific tools which highly skilled tool and die makers make for particular jobs. This is where I first began to understand, in a sensuous and matter-of-fact way, that we — human beings — are creators and not merely users of tools. Doing the tedious labor of a lathe hand, I saw that in creating the specific tools to deal with a difficult engineering situation, people could actually retool matters. There, in that sub-sub-basement machine shop, my commitment to practicalism — to building rather than to theorizing — took root.

From the shop I went to Korea — this was just at the tail end of the war — to serve in the U.S. infantry. Thanks to the G.I. Bill, after Korea I went back to City College to complete my bachelor's degree. From there I went to Stanford University, which is where I eventually received a Ph.D. in philosophy and methodology.

At Stanford I became interested in the study of language as a tool, especially mental and emotional language — how we talk (and that we talk) about our beliefs and feelings — and in the philosophical assumptions that shape such talking. Once I began teaching at colleges and universities, I recognized that there was a crucial connection between emotionality and learning. I saw that emotional "blocks," for example, often interfere with the learning process, holding it back or otherwise distorting it — a fact that has very important implications for the relationship between learning and development. Building environments (creating, like a tool and die maker, specific tools) with which that relationship is organized so that learning and development are unified is the ongoing activity of the social therapeutic approach to therapy and to education. Creativity is what I love most about sports. When I was younger — particularly at Stanford in the early '60s — I spent many hours hanging around ballfields and running tracks, watching and occasionally working out with athletes — some of them enormously talented, world-class, and others (like me) just guys from the streets — who were playing for the joy of it. As a lifelong sports nut, I'm increasingly able to appreciate the sheer beauty of people playing together, particularly as I grow older and become less vulnerable to feeling that I have to root for "my" team.

Which brings me back to that imaginary quality called "wisdom." As I see it, there's very little about wisdom that's creative, playful, or joyous. Wisdom is something that old people, and people who are "wise beyond their years," supposedly have. Once you've got it, presumably, it sits there in your brain and never develops because — it's Wisdom. "Wise" people never change their minds, or anything else. I don't have any wisdom, thank you, and with any luck I never will.

What I do have is some practical expertise in helping people to develop. It's been my experience that exercising (physically, intellectually, emotionally) is developmental, so at the end of each chapter you'll see one or more "emotional exercises" that I think you may find helpful. You might also like to make up some of your own. Whatever you do, don't turn them into golden rules. Don't make the mistake of confusing expertise with wisdom.

Unlike many of the people who became active in the '60s, I have remained an activist. For many years I have been deeply involved in the movement to build an inclusive, independent, national third party in America as part of an even broader effort to democratize the political process. In politics, as in life, I believe that it's always healthier for people to make what there is to make with whatever is available than "to make the best of it." A new politics for a new century is also, as I see it, a toolmaking task.

I believe very deeply in democracy, in people working together to make it happen — at the polling booth, on the basketball court, in the bedroom, in the classroom, at the workplace, in the therapy office and everywhere else. I don't believe in obeying, or being, an Authority Figure. So there's nothing in this book that's intended to put down anyone's beliefs, religious or otherwise. I do think we all need to raise questions about how we want to live our lives, given what we believe. It's healthy, in my opinion, when we allow ourselves to run the risk of having our deepest beliefs challenged — but everyone needs to decide for himself and herself whether, and how, to do that and, ultimately, what to do with it.

Let's Develop! is, among other things, a story book. The stories are of some of the thousands of ordinary people from all walks of life who've been part of my therapy practice over the last quarter of a century. These folks have allowed me into their lives; they've shared their humiliation, their fear, their pain and their joy with me. I love them all very deeply. Now, through this book, they continue to give. They are my heroines and heroes and it is to them that this book is dedicated.

Social therapy, the approach presented in *Let's Develop!*, grows out of many sources. A most important influence is the Austrian-born philosopher Ludwig Wittgenstein, considered by many to be the greatest philosopher of the 20th century, who taught that "the solution of the problem of life is seen in the vanishing of the problem." Working to make the problem "vanish" — indeed, to deny that there is a problem to be solved, to challenge practically the "problem-solution" worldview by creating new kinds of tools — is very much the practice of the social therapeutic method.

Lev Vygotsky, the Russian psychologist who did such extraordinary research work in the '20s and early '30s (he died of tuberculosis in 1934, at the age of 38) and whose writings have only recently become available again, also understood that "life is not a problem"; it is an activity. Only if it is lived as an activity, he insisted, can it be developmental. To live life as an activity we must work together to complete what each of us is doing rather than to compete with each other.

The Vygotskian notion of completion is critical to a proper understanding of speaking and writing and language acquisition as activity. For we do not simply use language as a tool. We are tool makers. We create language by engaging in the activity of speaking. Thinking and feeling are likewise activities inextricably connected to speaking and writing. Talking to each other is as much writing a poem together as it is conveying information.

Phyllis Goldberg and I completed this book together. While I take ultimate responsibility for the "strange" — although I believe useful — ideas contained in it, Phyllis, a dear friend and colleague, was with me all the way in the book's creation. A brilliant thinker and the world's funniest "feminist," she ceaselessly helped me to move beyond my own resistance to writing a "pop" psychology book.

Please be outraged by it. If you do not throw it against the wall at least five times during the reading of it, I will be disappointed.

— *Fred Newman*
New York City
July 1994

Let's Develop!

1

Giving in a Culture of Getting

Whether or not we believe in the abstract that it's more blessed to give than to receive, in our everyday lives most of us are practitioners (more or less successful) of getting. Getting is not only a totally legitimate activity in our culture, it's highly valued. People who are good at getting (the go-getters) are admired and rewarded. Those who aren't often become objects of pity or blame; they don't "get it," they're losers, unhip, failures.

We are trained from early childhood to play the getting game. The object of the game is to get as much as you can while giving as little as you can. Although you can't expect to get something for nothing, the rules of the game say that you give only in order to get. Giving more than you get, or giving anything away if you can get something for it, is a sign of poor judgment — or worse.

Now many of us make a distinction between those areas of life in which the getting game seems to be perfectly appropriate and reasonable, and those in which it is considered something between impolite and morally wrong. Economic life, for example, is explicitly organized on the basis of the getting principle; making a profit is what our economy is about. Working for a living, shopping for a bargain, selling to the highest bidder, buying shares to receive dividends, are the recognized terms of the American social/economic contract.

Personal life, however, is — at least in principle — quite different. Here, wheeling and dealing — not to mention buying and selling — are often regarded as crude or immoral (and sometimes illegal, too). The teenage boy who expects a girl to "put out" on their first date in return for being "taken out," and the woman who sells sex on the street corner, are both acting from the same profit motive (the getting principle) that inspires everyone from the grocer down the block to the chairman of the board, as well as everyone who's ever bought a lottery ticket, punched a time clock or claimed a tax deduction for making a charitable contribution. But date rape and prostitution are considered wrong in our culture; personal life is expected to be organized not around the getting principle but on the basis of feelings. This is true not only of sexual relationships, but of friendships and the relationships between parents and children.

Yet the division between economic life and personal life is sometimes not all that clear. Ordinary activities — including those we do with the people we care the most about — are deeply imbued with the philosophy of getting. They're unofficially contractual. ("I'll do this for you if you do this for me.") They're gratuitously competitive. ("I'm a better parent — or friend, or lover, or woman, or mourner — than you are." "I try harder — or feel things more deeply, or pay more attention, or put up with much worse — than you do.") They're acquisitive. ("I have to have you!" "You owe me that much.")

The getting principle is so much a part of our culture and, therefore, "in us" that most of the time we aren't even aware that it organizes our relationships with other human beings; it's not possible just to leave it behind at the office or the shop. It's even in our language. How we speak to one another — not just what we say, but the way we say it — is one of the most powerful ways in which the competitive, contractual, acquisitive mode that characterizes the culture of getting is expressed and reinforced.

The societally acceptable form of good conversation in our culture is typically an exchange, a trade: you tell me your ideas, your feelings, your experiences, and then it's my turn to tell you mine. We listen to each other just long enough and attentively enough to make the connection — "Oh! That makes me think of...my childhood, the last time I was sick, my favorite movie star..." — so that we can have our turn at getting (attention, admiration, respect).

Now it turns out that the culture of getting sometimes fails people, even by their own standards. Competitiveness and acquisitiveness may serve Mr. Money well in the boardroom, but it's not so clear that they make for success in the bedroom — or any of the other places where we live our lives. Ironically, people who, like Mr. Money, organize their lives on the basis of the getting principle — which means many or most of us — often are more or less deprived, emotionally disadvantaged, and underdeveloped. (I am making a distinction here between being undeveloped, as children are when they haven't yet grown to their full height, and being underdeveloped, as people are when their growth has been stunted as the result of malnourishment, disease or injury.) Of course, this doesn't look exactly the same for everyone: men and women, people from various ethnic backgrounds and social classes, all do different versions of getting — and how they do it has a big impact on their emotional lives. But the culture of getting is something we all participate in. It's part of our shared culture.

The point I'm making is not that getting is immoral. It's simply that, like cholesterol, in many life situations getting isn't very good for our (emotional) health. We may not die from it. But it puts us at constant risk.

One of the most important principles of the social therapeutic approach is that although we live in a culture of getting, people are helped much more — emotionally and developmentally — by giving than they are by getting. What I mean by giving is the active sharing of all our emotional "possessions" — including, in the appropriate environments, our pathology, our pain and our humiliation.

Learning to be accepting — letting other people be giving to you — is a very important corollary of the giving principle. Letting people give to you isn't the same as getting; in fact it's actually a kind of giving.

The social therapeutic approach helps people to break out of the getting mode, to put aside the getting principle (where appropriate) in favor of a more sophisticated and gratifying method for living. The people who are most helped by the social therapeutic approach are those who allow themselves to learn how to make giving the organizing principle of their emotional lives. They usually do so with conflicts, of course — which is perfectly fine.

For one thing, as I've said, being unusually giving violates a fundamental principle of our culture. So people tend to worry, not surprisingly, that they'll be ripped off. In our culture of getting, people are getting ripped off, emotionally speaking and otherwise, much of the time. If you give more than usual, there's the concern that you'll be the victim — ripped off — more than usual. Paradoxically, it's only when you're unconditionally giving emotionally that you can't get ripped off at all. (Someone named Jesus said that!) What's more, the more you give, the less time you have to spend and the less mental energy you have to exert worrying that you'll be ripped off or resenting that you have been. What a relief! Ironically, many people feel degraded by being related to as having something to give emotionally when they "know," or believe "deep down," that they have nothing to give. A culture of getting tends to undermine our sense of self-worth. After all, when you're spending almost every waking moment frenetically trying to get all you can, your "subconscious" might well be thinking that you must not have very much — that you're missing something. At the same time, the assumption that people do have something to give often makes them angry because it challenges their life strategy of trying to get all the time. It challenges their societal identity as a high-powered getter.

Then there are those people who have a kind of "martyr complex" — they seem to get off on not getting. Most of us have at least one person in our lives who's like this. Some of their favorite phrases are: "Oh, don't worry about me…" "No, thank you…" "I don't want anything…" "It doesn't matter…" "I'll be fine…" "Go ahead without me…" and "Whatever you say…" It's very, very difficult to be giving to them. They're often rejecting; they seem to take pride in not needing or wanting anything or anyone. And they typically adopt an attitude of moral superiority, as if they were better than the rest of us because they prefer to do without. In fact they're into getting too; they're into getting nothing.

How do people who have been socialized in the culture of getting come to see themselves as having something to give? By giving. They give, and in doing so they discover that they have something to give — not the other way around. We don't know how to do it, nor that we can do it, in advance — how could we?

The social therapeutic approach teaches people to create environments where emotional giving is practiced — environments in which people are supported and encouraged to practice a way of living ("living as giving") that is different from what we are used to in our getting culture. Our culture of getting is economically very sophisticated but emotionally simplistic and crude. We live in a world where many, many people (across all ethnic, racial and gender lines) are emotionally undeveloped, underdeveloped and "uncultured."

What this means is that many adults don't know how to do much emotionally, or to do things differently from what they did when they were children first learning to adapt to society and didn't get their way, or didn't get what they wanted, or didn't get as much as someone else got. Most of us have the emotions that got "handed out" to everyone at the beginning. Along the way we may have refined those emotions slightly, but typically we haven't created any new ones. Most of us don't even know that this is something people can do. But, to paraphrase William Shakespeare, there are more emotions in heaven and earth than are dreamt of in our getting culture — or in traditional psychology.

As a social therapist, I will say to someone, up front (and you could say something like this too): "Look, the reason that you're responding in that way isn't because you're a bad person, but because you're emotionally ignorant. You're emotionally very limited. All you know how to do is slug people (verbally or physically) who offend you, or insult them, or make fun of them. Do you want to learn how to do something different?" It's not simply a moral issue. It's a developmental issue.

In creating a social therapeutic environment, people participate in an emotionally more "advanced" and creative culture of giving. The social therapeutic approach adds tools to people's emotional repertoire; it gives them more emotional options, including the significant option of creating brand-new emotions. It's like mixing paints. There are some basic colors. But the possibilities for new colors are endless.

Again, it's not merely a matter of morality — although I do take the moral position that people should have as many emotional options, as many emotional alternatives, as possible. Social therapy teaches people to create environments inside and outside the therapy office where a different emotional culture (creating new emotions) is practiced. Take a situation (all too common in our culture) in which a man is getting ready to hit his wife. He's storming around the house, the children are terrified, the wife is crying. Social therapy teaches him that (and how) he could hold her hand instead! He could alter his rigid societal posture, which has become second nature to him but is in fact what he has learned in the getting culture about how to be a man, how to be angry, how to get (his revenge, his satisfaction, his pride back).

"Hey, man! I know you don't want to! But you could. You can do better than saying, 'I couldn't help myself.' By changing your cultural posture, by challenging your cultural role, by giving rather than getting — by mixing a new emotion — you could no longer be in a position to hurt her." Such a small (actually, not so small) change, such a cultural variation, such a shift in nuance, such a momentary breaking out of our societally overdetermined roles, could make all the difference in the world. It changes everything.

Or take touching. Many people (men and women alike) assume that if they don't feel like being touched at a particular moment then they also wouldn't want to touch the person they are with. But the giving of touching is a very different activity from getting touched. Now if you're only into getting, or giving to get, that's not really an option. (It's more like a waste of time, or a chore, or a "favor.") But if you're into giving, it isn't any of those things.

The social therapeutic approach reorganizes our culturally limited emotionality. Everyday sexism, homophobia, racism and the other "isms" are as much the products of the culture of getting as they are expressions of how the economy and politics are organized. In the absence of creating a new emotional culture, there doesn't seem to me to be much hope of doing a whole lot about them. *Change* the cultural/emotional environment, and the "isms" that thrive in the culture of getting will lack nourishment and, in my opinion, they'll begin to die.

Taking courses in art or music or a foreign language, or traveling, often gives us a greater aesthetic sensibility, broadens our perspective, enhances our ability to appreciate and to create beauty. Social therapy makes people more "cultured" and developed emotionally. It challenges our emotional underdevelopment. The social therapeutic approach teaches people that when someone screams at you there are other things to do besides screaming back — just as people who study painting learn that there is more to the visual arts than a coloring book and a box of Crayolas. This is what we mean by saying that social therapy is a culturally transforming experience. It teaches us a new, and developmental, way of seeing things and creating a new life. It's about the "re-mixing" of our lives.

EXERCISES:

Here's something you can try out which may give you a more focused look at what giving feels like.

Be unexpectedly giving — for "no reason at all" — to someone who's unlikely to give you anything in return.

———

Here are a few ways to practice "mixing new emotions."

1. Add a little silliness to a situation you're not usually silly in.

2. Get a kick out of finding out that you made a mistake about something.

3. Fall in love anew with someone you already love.

2

Stop Behaving!

Rose is a 66-year-old woman who came into social therapy because she felt that she was "just going through the motions" of her life. According to her husband, Sam, Rose "has everything" — a beautiful home, a new car, expensive clothes. But Rose feels that her home is a "prison," especially since she and Sam sold their prosperous business.

Sam has never physically harmed Rose, or even threatened to. But she's afraid of him anyway. She's afraid to ask a "stupid" question when they're watching the news, or to "make a mistake" when she's driving, or to express one of her "ridiculous" opinions. When their son and daughter-in-law visit, Rose says, it "kills" her to see Sam "push them away" with his bullying and sarcasm. Rose once told her social therapy group that she tries to remember "what it was like" to like her husband, but she can't even imagine it.

When Rose said that, another woman in the group, Laura, got very upset. Laura is a social worker; her husband Richard teaches political science at a prestigious university. They're both in their early thirties and successful in their careers. Laura decided to take a six-month leave of absence just before their child was born. She welcomed the chance to stay home for a while, especially because Richard works at home a lot. It didn't turn out as she expected. "I feel as if I'm invisible," she told us. "Richard's polite about the baby, the way a stranger might be. Sometimes I think he wishes we would both just go away."

It's miserable to be poor in the financial sense — to have to go without, and to see your family go without, what you all need in order to live comfortably. Whether or not we have the material necessities of life is very, very important. But that isn't all there is.

I have come to believe that to live without feeling wanted or welcome, without being looked at or attended to, without giving or receiving smiles, kisses, small kindnesses and encouragement, makes people just as deprived. To live without experiencing intensity and excitement in your everyday life — to live without joy, day after day, year after year — is as deadening to the human spirit as it is to live without having enough food to eat or a roof over your head.

I think that joy is one of life's necessities. I'm not advocating the "pleasure principle" here — living life for the purpose of having a good time, pursuing a psychological "pop" or a drug-induced "high" from every moment. I'm talking about the ongoing experience of choosing how you want to be living and liking the choices that you make.

Sadly, there are many, many people like Rose and Laura, who spend much of their lives doing what they don't want to be doing — "going through the motions" without seeing any reason to, but feeling that they're "obligated" to keep doing it. They believe that this is what "real" life is about — "mature," "responsible" people not only make their beds but lie in them (however lumpy they may be); fulfilling their obligations is the important thing, no matter what the emotional cost. And they feel trapped.

Most of the men and women who come into social therapy

are, like Rose and Laura, ordinary people who are leading halfway decent lives. They aren't materially deprived. They're not "failures" by societal standards — they have good jobs, stable families, and friends.

And they feel trapped! They don't like what they're doing — not just at particular times or on particular days, but most of the time. What they're saying about their lives is this: I don't enjoy what I'm doing. This is not something I want to be doing. I don't know why I'm here.

Sometimes religion, or morality, is invoked to justify staying in a life situation that's miserable in this way. But in my experience as a therapist, it's usually the case that people with a religious faith or a set of moral precepts that sustains them do feel that their lives are satisfying and worthwhile because of that. Their beliefs inform and shape everything they do. They don't need to use religion and morality "after the fact" to justify their misery because they aren't miserable. It's when people don't have anything in their lives to turn to that religious or ethical values are most likely to be "dragged in" to keep them "in their place." And that, in my opinion, is neither religious nor moral. It's abusive.

People like Rose and Laura feel their lives are empty because — as a result of circumstance, or choices they've made — they've wound up in non-developmental (which means anti-developmental) life situations. They're acting out bad roles in a bad play. They've given up — an easy thing to do when you don't know that as a human being you can choose to live your life differently, that is, that you have the capacity to develop.

Not knowing that you have the capacity for unlimited development is, in essence, not knowing that you're human. That's why the experience of it is so horrible.

When people allow their lives to be completely determined by societal rules and categories, they're engaging in "conditioned behavior" — the automatic acts in response to environmental "stimuli" that were made famous by Professor Pavlov's dog. As I've often pointed out in lectures and articles, the problem with behaviorism as a theory isn't that it's wrong but that it's right! In a coercive societal environment, human beings do indeed give up our humanness — our unique capacity for creative activity. Instead, we behave as passive objects which can only be acted upon. This has nothing to do with "brainwashing," by the way, as some self-appointed experts insist. It's the product of societal coercion. Sadly, it is normal behavior. And the more coercive the societal environment, the more likely people are to behave rather than to create.

In human beings, behavior is both the producer and the product of abuse. I'm not just talking about the abuse that's making the headlines these days — child abuse, sexual abuse, domestic violence — the kind that causes visible damage and can be reported as a crime. I'm talking here about abusive behavior that's less extreme — that is, it doesn't leave any marks — and for this very reason is in some ways more pernicious. It's often imperceptible to the naked eye, or ear, so many people tend not to see or hear it for what it is. Thousands of small brutal acts are perpetrated day in and day out by people who "honestly" can't see that they're being abusive to people who "honestly" can't see that they're being abused. I call this Abusive Behavior Syndrome.

From the vantage point of the social therapeutic approach, the only way to stop Abusive Behavior Syndrome is to stop behavior. Social therapy does not try to help people to "modify" their behavior. Rather, we help people to break out of their societally overdetermined behavior patterns and to become the active creators of their lives.

You see, it is as much in our nature as human beings to perform creatively as to behave. Behavior is what all other living things do. As far as anyone has been able to tell, it's all they can do. Beavers, for example, do many interesting things. But they don't write, produce and direct theatrical pieces. What I am calling performance — the conscious activity of producing how we are in the world — is unique to our species. While behavior is dehumanizing, performance is developmental.

Remember the man in Chapter 1 who could, at the very moment he was about to hit his wife, do something "a little bit" different and take her hand instead?

His awareness that he could — not necessarily would — stop behaving raises the issue of how he's living his life. I'm not some authority figure who's saying to him, in the name of Morality (with a capital M) or Humanity (with a capital H), that "in theory" he could stop. I'm saying: "You can do another thing right now! You can be something other than a prefabricated, mass-produced product of the male role! These societal roles are not all that's available to us. Let's turn your life into a play that you direct! Don't just change this behavior — this line, or this scene — create a whole new life!"

From the social therapeutic point of view, in fact, the thing that's least likely to change is particular behavior. Behavior modification — a highly coercive technique to help people stop doing all kinds of things from drinking to smoking cigarettes to "overeating" — has been a conspicuous failure.

What's most possible in those moments of acute self-awareness is to transform your entire life. You can say to yourself — Wait a minute! Who am I? What am I doing with my life? I must be engaged in a profound denial of my humanness to behave in this way. It has nothing to do with any decision I ever made about the kind of human being I want to be. Where am I in deciding what my life is about? I don't have to live that way. I can transform my life!

This small moment, which can lead you to change everything, has to happen many times throughout the day, every day. It has to be your moment-to-moment life experience, your life performance.

EXERCISE:

Practice performing your life:

The next time you find yourself in a familiar situation (visiting your family, taking a coffee break with your co-workers, being at the movies with your Saturday night date), don't behave — perform!

3

The Problem with Solutions

People come to social therapy with every kind of "problem," including every kind of sexual "problem." They have a hard time having an orgasm. They're afraid that they're "oversexed." They're "reluctant virgins." They ejaculate "prematurely." They can't have an erection. They think that their breasts are too big. They worry that their penises are too small...

You can imagine their surprise when they learn that we don't try to solve sexual "problems" — or any other kind of "problem," for that matter. The social therapeutic approach doesn't make use of a "problem"-"solution" framework, because we don't believe it's very useful.

What's more (get ready for another surprise), we're not attempting to make people better at sex! Which isn't to say that it's impossible to get better at sex. Certainly, all kinds of things — transactional skills, a sexy nightgown, transcendental meditation, one or two glasses of wine, talking to a good friend or, most importantly, to your sexual partner — can be useful for that purpose, and some of them can actually be quite helpful. I think you should try out whatever you think might work for you and your partner. The social therapeutic approach supports people to make moves, without prescribing what moves they ought (or ought not) to make.

Our approach to sexual "problems" will help you to see, I think, that the best way to help people is not to diagnose their "problems" — or try to come up with "solutions" — at all.

From the social therapeutic vantage point, playing how very young children play isn't just for kids. It's a way that grownups can create all kinds of things, from art to intimacy. So we work hard to teach people how to play (again). What I mean by this is teaching them how to build environments, out of whatever is at hand, in which they can be playful. A friend of mine remembers her four-year-old self dragging economy-size cans of sardines out of her mother's cupboard, which she would attach to her feet with rubber bands; she says she had the most marvelous time stomping around the house on her "stilts." Learning how to play again in this way must include learning how to deal with whatever it is that keeps you from doing it. Such playful environments aren't merely a precondition for playing, nor are they the result of playing. They're both, at the same time. One of the games adults may decide to play in these environments is sex.

I think that at its best, sex is a way of playing for grownups. I'm not talking about the "games people play" kind of transactional sex that mirrors all too well the culture of getting. When sex is turned into those kinds of highly rule-governed games, it's likely to be aggressive. ("Give it to me!") It's most likely to be competitive. ("Am I the best you've ever had?") It's most likely to be commodified. ("How much will you give me for giving this to you?") And what people do when they're playing the contractual sex game is most likely to be read as a sign, or a symbol, of what it "means" rather than allowed to be what it is. ("He didn't have an erection with me because he's seeing someone else." "If you loved me, you would.")

I'm talking about a very different kind of playing — and a very different kind of sex. What social therapy means by playing is closer to playing the way very young children do, before they learn to play rule-governed games. Playing in early childhood isn't characteristically governed by rules which are known and understood beforehand (as in baseball and hopscotch, or Scrabble and Clue). Rather, the rules (insofar as there are any) are created in the context of playing — they're made up as the players go along, as much to describe what they are doing as to prescribe what they are allowed to do.

Very little children play just for the fun of it. Their playing doesn't have a beginning, a middle or an end. It typically isn't "for" any purpose. It doesn't "mean" anything. In this kind of playing, no one scores. You can't be "good" or "bad" at it — or "too fat" or "too small" to play. There are no winners and losers, no trophies and no booby prizes.

This is not in any way to trivialize sex, to suggest that anything goes, or to imply that it's something people can or should do with any old body. Sex without intimacy, in my opinion, tends to be the most aggressive, the most competitive, the most "store-bought" and "ready-made." It comes complete with prefabricated rules, roles and meanings that predetermine almost everything about it, from who can play to the "object" of the game (or what you have to do in order to beat your opponent).

No, the best kind of sex, in my view, the sex in which there's the least amount of pretense — the most gratifying and satisfying sex — is sex you do with the person (or people) in your life with whom you are most open. That way the players can let their hair down and just play — freely, gaily — unencumbered by rigid rules that were made up before you ever lay down to play, unburdened by the meanings that are imposed on us in the culture of getting.

It's not a means to an end, but something you do because you both want to. Sex is at its very best, I believe, when you're playing at it with a best friend — not just another "consenting adult," but someone you care about and who cares about you.

Well, all that sounds very nice, you may be thinking. *But what about those deep bio-social sexual problems you were talking about before? Where do they come in?*

They don't! The social therapeutic approach doesn't treat or try to solve problems because we don't think there are such things. *No such thing as problems?* That's right — just as there's no such thing as unicorns, or talking animals. You can imagine them, believe in them, give them names and even tell fascinating stories about them, but...there ain't no such (horn-y or talk-y) creatures.

Okay, you might say. *But if there aren't any problems, then what is there? And if there aren't any unicorns or talking animals, then what is there?* Good questions. The answer is that there is life. Life in all its rich complexity, contradictoriness, up-and-down, chaotic, all-at-onceness — life that we as human beings are uniquely the movers and shakers, creators and makers of. You remember us — the ones who made up the unicorns and the talking animals!

The problem with problems is that they are the product of a method, a model, which has proven highly useful to our species over the last several hundred years or so in transforming the natural world but, as I see it, is neither relevant nor particularly helpful when it is applied to (imposed on) human life. It's one thing to identify as a problem a boulder that's blocking the path to the river and to decide that removing it is the best solution. It's another thing entirely to identify, or define, or diagnose human life in terms of a static, non-developmental, uncreative problem-solution paradigm.

Identifying some aspect or dimension or activity of human life as a "problem" turns it into a thing, arbitrarily separating it out from the multidimensional, seamless wholeness of life. It reduces life to an endless series of "boulders" and to the search for techniques that will get them off the path so that everything returns to "normal." The problem-solution paradigm becomes not only a way of life, but a substitute for it.

Social therapy is not anti-technique. We encourage people to make use of whatever techniques are available that they think will be helpful to them. At the same time, we teach people to create techniques — which includes creating the environments where the creation of techniques is supported. This, of course, is very different from the traditional therapeutic enterprise of teaching people only to use the techniques that are already there.

You see, human beings are not just users of hardware store tools; we are also toolmakers. To relate to people as if all they are capable of doing is using what exists is, from the social therapeutic point of view, anti-developmental; it excludes the creative dimension of human life. Social therapy helps people to be better creators of their lives, which includes the continuous development of techniques for living. We work to help people create a cultural environment in which the uniquely human capacity for invention is encouraged. And, so far as I'm concerned, every human being is creative.

In our society, where everything from aging to "static cling" is identified as a "problem" and there's always a "solution" for sale, it's easy to get caught in the problem-solution trap.

Obesity is a good example of how some aspect of a person's life that may need to be worked on, or dealt with, gets turned into a thing-in-itself. That obsession, combined with the never-ending search for a "solution" (dieting being notoriously unsuccessful in solving this "problem"), often becomes a substitute for life. I think Susan Powter is understandably a heroine to so many because she has raised her voice on behalf of the millions of women who have been bullied into abandoning their lives for dieting.

There's substantial evidence that people who weigh more or

less than they would like to, or than is healthy for them, aren't particularly aware of the way they carry out many life activities — including eating. This is not in any way to blame people for being "overweight" or for drinking "too much," or for "doing" drugs. The point I'm making is that the problem-solution paradigm, by turning eating or drinking or drug use into a thing-in-itself, makes it extremely difficult for people to transform the totality of their lives — which includes the activity of putting food and other substances into their bodies, but isn't limited to that. No matter what, or how much, we eat or drink or smoke or whatever, we all still have to decide how we're going to organize our lives as a whole — what work we do, who our friends are, where we live, which games we play.

The message here is this: if you want to change anything in your life, you have to change your whole life. And it turns out that changing your whole life is far easier than changing particular things in it.

The social therapeutic approach teaches people to recreate the totality of their lives continuously — to take responsibility for being the active agents and organizers of the whole rich complexity of their life activities. We teach people to create environments that aren't "problem"-oriented but development-oriented. It's in building such environments that people learn how to engage in the continuous, creative activity of living their lives rather than in the circular and futile one of "solving" their "problems."

Ironically, this is why we've been able to be so effective in helping people to get off drugs — we never work on the "problem" of drug use. Moreover, we never relate to people in terms of their "identities" as "drug addicts" or "alcoholics" or anything else, for that matter. We don't label life — we help people to live it.

Many traditional therapeutic approaches tend to put people with the same "problems" — "overweight," "addiction," sexual trauma

— in their own groups. Particularly in the case of "problems" that are associated with moral inferiority, the assumption is that the "bad," "ugly" people who have them shouldn't impose themselves — and their "problems" — on the "nice" people with whom they supposedly have nothing in common. However, I don't believe there's much evidence to indicate that separating people in this way, according to their "problems," is very effective.

There is plenty of evidence to show that people from all walks of life who use drugs are not fundamentally different from people who have other "problems." We've also discovered, over the last 25 years, that people get an enormous amount of help from people who are *other* — who were brought up with other values, who come from other ethnic backgrounds and other walks of life, who are in other life circumstances.

We've found that people often learn to see who they are by interacting with people who aren't so much the same. It's kind of like looking in a mirror — what you see when you look at your reflection (which, after all, is not you) is not what you see when you look at yourself, but how you look to other people; that's why mirrors can be so useful. You can do this in your own life by making a practice of relating to people — in your family, on your street, at your job — who are different from you.

Social therapy groups are made as heterogeneous as possible: women and men, gay people and straight people, people of color and white people, working class and middle class people, older people and younger people, are all in groups with each other. The basis for them to work together in social therapy is not their common "identity" but their shared capacity as human beings — as life builders — for unlimited development. In fact, we work to help people break the "identity" habit altogether — including the habit of identifying people as "men," "women," "gay," "straight," "Black," "white," "working class," "middle class," "old," "young" — to see what they can create together with their differences rather than assuming what they can and cannot do together based on the faulty premise of identity. In other words, the social therapeutic approach is most attentive to what people do — to their activity — and not to the "explanatory" identifying labels that people superimpose on that activity, constraining and deforming it.

I'm not just speaking here of societally disapproved or negative identities, by the way. I'm talking about how identity — as a primary means of understanding and relating to ourselves and other people — has a negative impact on development, regardless of how valued particular identities (parent, clergyman, judge) might be.

"Mother," for example, comes out of the highly complex set of social, economic, biological, cultural and political activities which include bearing and rearing a child. While it is considered to be a positive identity in our culture (as it is in most others), it is also used to categorize, limit and control the people — nearly always women — who carry those mothering activities out. They are required to be Mothers (with a capital M) and to behave in Motherly ways. If they don't, they're heavily penalized for it. This process makes it very hard for them to do mothering creatively — although it does make Mothers easier to explain (and make judgments about) — and very hard for men to do mothering at all.

Explanations are part of the extended family of Labels that include Identity and the Problem-Solution "twins." Like other Labels, Explanations also help to undermine development. Where does labeling, including explaining, come from? You might be tempted to think that it's "only natural" for human beings to stick a Label on everything and everyone: He has an "inferiority complex," she has an "eating disorder," their child is "hyperactive"; I'm an "alcoholic," you're a "compulsive shopper," and our child is an "underachiever" with a "high IQ" and "low self-esteem." In fact, however, Labels are fairly recent arrivals on the societal scene.

Over the last three centuries, the extraordinary accomplishments of the physical sciences made labeling — their standard operating procedure — seem to be just what psychology needed.

The assumption was that we, human beings, can understand ourselves by using the same methods which are used so effectively to understand the natural world: stars, trees, rocks, birds and bees. The problem (if you'll pardon the expression) with that assumption is that — as far as we know — stars have never made up a star psychology, nor have rocks or trees made up their own psychologies, nor have birds or bees attempted to create a psychology for themselves.

Although there may be general laws that account for the movement of stars, the formation of rocks, the growth of trees, the mating habits of birds and the social organization of bees, those laws were discovered by human beings about the natural world. The objects that the laws of physics are about — molecules and quanta (the very small "parcels" that make up many forms of energy) — don't make up the laws; physicists do. By contrast, the "laws" of psychology are made up by human beings about human beings. Those pseudo-laws are fundamentally and essentially informed, and deformed, by this subjectivity. In other words, we are both the studiers and the studied.

This basic fact of life, in my view, makes the scientific model inapplicable and irrelevant to human life. Moreover, the "laws" of traditional psychology, distorted by subjectivity, weigh us down and keep us from growing. They box us in; they don't allow us to live our lives as richly and as creatively as we could.

You see, the life of our species is far more emergent than is accounted for by traditional psychology's so-called scientific "laws." What I mean by this is simply that a great deal of what happens in human life — in its "smallest," most ordinary moments and at its most dramatic junctures — just doesn't fit into the preexisting patterns and paradigms that psychologists call "laws." These "happenings" are much closer to cultural creations than they are to the "timeless" discoveries of the physical sciences. Let me put it this way: Albert Einstein could rediscover physics (including its subjective relativity) to account for the nature of matter, but no number of psychological Insights could account for the emergent phenomenon of Albert Einstein.

Insights are part of the prevailing scientific, "objective" mode of understanding. They're not used to transform rule-governed, role-governed environments, but to "illuminate" them. They are, supposedly, among the means by which we subjectively know (and "discover") patterns; they are, literally, a "seeing into" what already exists.

Now it's not that I'm opposed to insights (with a small *i*); every now and then we even have an insight in social therapy! But I do think we need to examine how they're used, in therapy and in everyday life. There's not much evidence that Insights (or insights) help us to reorganize the activity of living our lives — although they may make how we think about our lives more interesting. From a social therapeutic (developmental) point of view, something can be insightful and yet be of no value whatsoever.

Like its paradigmatic relatives (Explanations and the rest), Insights satisfy our culturally driven need to make sense of the world — our culturally evolved assumption that we need to have an Explanation for everything. But what if there is no Explanation for why your father drank, or why you married your high school sweetheart, or why your son hates broccoli? What if there are no Explanations, period? The social therapeutic approach helps people to live their lives creatively — not to understand, explain, interpret or otherwise label their lives as a prerequisite for, or an alternative to, living.

I don't believe that dreams, for example, reveal "underlying truths" about the people who dream them, or "deeper mental processes" that take place unbeknownst to the dreamer. Rather, it seems to me that dreams are like plays, which people "write" during one of the times when we tend to be less constrained by the demands of an awake, institutionalized, fully "mobilized" culture. We make up the plot, breathe imaginative life into the characters, give them their gestures, their costumes and their lines, and bring down the curtain at the end. And we don't necessarily remember all of that, just as we don't remember all kinds of other things we create in the course of our days and nights. Dreaming is a creative human activity; social therapists are interested in it as we are interested in everything else that people create. But I don't know of any evidence, Sigmund Freud notwithstanding, to show that dreams contain a secret code which only a professional interpreter of dreams can decipher to get at "privileged information" about the dreamer which he or she supposedly doesn't or can't know; I don't think there's any such information to be known. It seems to me that who people are, and what we create, is just that — who we are and what we create.

Which isn't to say that there are no patterns, no regularity in human life — merely that there's at least as much that's unexpected, that's unaccountable for. Moreover, the patterns and regularities are themselves shaped, and mis-shaped, by human subjectivity, which "selects" them out of the seamless wholeness of our lives.

Life is a dynamic relationship between what is to be expected and what is new. The kindred concepts of Problems, Solutions, Identity and Explanation and all their relatives leave out that emergent dimension of life. They effectively deny that people are the creators and — in the case of psychology — the subjects of patterns. In doing so, they hold back our quintessentially human capacity to create, to make the world anew continuously, to develop.

Traditional psychology, like language itself, has adopted the metaphysical (mystical and mystifying) bias of science and religion. It splits life into the opposing realms of visible, "surface" things and invisible, "underlying" secrets, with Explanations and Insights as the intermediaries between the two: a child having a tantrum is really "asking for attention," a woman who eats a lot is really "hungry for affection," a man who likes kung fu movies is really "insecure about his masculinity."

Psychology talks about life as if it were a fake painting that experts have to scrape to get to the "real" meanings underneath — which makes it difficult to talk about and see emotions as activities. But I think it's very important to do so. The first principle of traditional psychology, reinforced over and over again in ordinary language, is that it's necessary to go "more deeply into" things, to "get to the bottom." This principle is, in my opinion, a tremendous barrier to development because it assumes that life is static and unchanging rather than the product of continuous human activity. It is this metaphysical bias of psychology — not science, and not religion — that social therapy challenges.

EXERCISE:

Want to see what life would be like with no problems?

For one whole day, every time a problem comes up don't solve it — write a poem about it instead (even if you've never written a poem before).

4

The Man-Woman Thing

Frank is a handsome, good-natured man in his late thirties. A public interest lawyer, he's ambitious and very committed to his work; Frank sometimes becomes so preoccupied with a case that he's seemingly oblivious to what's going on around him. He's engaged to marry Jenny, a talented, vivacious, up-and-coming young actress whose career is also very important to her. Jenny is often furious with Frank for being "insensitive," "bossy" and "self-centered" — "sexist," for short.

One night, after having what Frank described to his social therapy group as "a nasty fight" with Jenny, he talked about their relationship. Frank said he feels that Jenny thinks he "just can't get it right" — and half the time he agrees with her. What about the rest of the time? Frank questions, he told us, whether he's really "the sexist creep she says I am" and resents it when Jenny gets sarcastic and "mean." According to Frank, Jenny thinks that everything he does is wrong. If he's that bad, and Jenny's that miserable, Frank said, he just doesn't understand what she's doing with him.

As a man, and as a therapist, I've learned an enormous amount from feminism. I'm not just talking about the *do*s and *don't*s that feminism is sometimes reduced to — although I do think that if you're going to go by any rules, the rules of feminism are usually fairer and more humane than the male-dominated rules they're intended to replace: Do pick up your dirty socks. Don't leave the toilet seat up. Do talk about your feelings. Don't tell her what to do. Do ask her what she thinks. Don't laugh at her opinions. Do find out what her sexual preferences are. Don't assume you know. And so on.

But much more significant than these rules, in my opinion, is the sensibility that modern feminism has contributed in the form of a very pointed and powerful critique of the male-dominated way of seeing and doing things. From a social therapeutic perspective, what's perhaps most important about feminism's critique is that the feminists dare to make it. In doing so, they challenge the status quo-biased assertion that male-centrism is simply the way things are. The feminist point is that male-centrism is neither neutral nor natural, but a profoundly biased way of seeing and doing things — a subjective "take" on the world.

The social therapeutic approach incorporates feminism in posing a radical challenge to the biases and assumptions embedded in male-dominated societal institutions, including, most critically, language. Yet while I have been heavily influenced by feminism, I do not call myself a "feminist." At best, it's pretentious for men to take credit for being on the "right side" where women are concerned. At worst, claiming feminism as a credential is yet another attempt by men, it seems to me, to rip women off — while simultaneously letting themselves off the hook should any women presume to criticize them, publicly or privately.

While feminism has had a profound influence on the social therapeutic approach, from my point of view the feminist critique of the male-dominated culture of getting is itself limited. For although feminism has correctly pointed out what's problematic in our culture, it has sometimes assumed that knowing what's wrong is likely to make things better.

Feminism still rests, it seems to me, on the '60s-ish liberal-radical methodology which suggests that social change can be brought about through something called "consciousness-raising." The assumption is that there's a thing, called consciousness, located (presumably) somewhere in people's heads, and that causing it to "rise" — for example, by teaching women that they are "oppressed" and men that they are "oppressors" — transforms their lives. But there's simply no evidence that such knowledge is, in and of itself, transformative. In fact, many people argue that since nothing is ever going to change, it's just as well not to be told what's wrong. By contrast, the social therapeutic approach insists that helping people to change their life activity is what changes how they think about it.

I do not question the validity of feminist theory. But in the absence of activity, any theory — even the best kind — doesn't go anywhere. Even more importantly, in the absence of activity *human beings* don't go anywhere. In other words, I am saying that feminism doesn't go far enough. With all due respect, I am being intentionally provocative here. I am questioning feminism's male-dominated method!

In social therapy we engage in the ongoing activity of deconstructing (taking apart and exposing the workings of) the culture of getting while simultaneously reconstructing a new culture of giving within it. We have discovered that participating in this activity and building the environment in which it takes place — the social therapy group, a friendship, a family — is profoundly developmental. And no small part of this activity is deconstructing and reconstructing how we talk — that is, language itself.

I think we often tend to forget that men and women are from two different "sub-cultures" (both within the culture of getting). They speak significantly different versions of the same language — not only do they not always mean the same thing by the words that they say, language itself doesn't mean the same thing to them. Their relationships to other societal institutions and arrangements — the family, sexuality, money, knowledge — are also different; and so, consequently, are many of their values and perceptions.

As anyone who's ever tried it knows, it isn't at all easy for men and women to build something together. And sometimes it's even harder than it needs to be because they don't know how, or aren't willing, to make use of everything they've got. Often this is true because they don't like what they've got. (This is especially true of women.)

I think it's important for men to hear what women are saying to them about how they need to be. Men have to be responsive to women's demands that they learn from women how to be more caring, how to be more thoughtful, and how to be more humane in their personal relationships. These are things women often know more about — not because of something in their genes, but because of who they've been brought up from childhood to be. If you, as a man, can learn to be sensitive to the issues that modern feminism has raised, you (not just the women in your life) will be one of the beneficiaries. Because to the extent that you learn to be more humane and decent, you can have closer, more intimate relationships with other people.

At the same time, men are who we are. That includes not only what we're able to learn but also who we've been brought up to be — men. This societal reality can't be denied, wished away or moralized out of existence.

I think that women have to make the demand that the men they're close to be decent...not only to them, but to other women, and to other men — to other human beings (including the Girl Scout who comes to the door selling cookies and the homeless old man you pass on your way to the movies). At the same time, women have to recognize and accept that men are...well, men.

In other words, a man and a woman need to be radically accepting of who each of them is in order to be intimate with one another. Radical acceptance produces intimacy — not the other way around. Moreover, radical acceptance is the starting point for growth and development; it is the putting aside of judgments to create a "guilt-free zone" in which people (in this case, a man and a woman) can give up their private ownership of whatever is humiliating to them.

In such an environment, men and women can support each other to break out of the sexist roles, and to break the sexist rules, that constrain and limit all of us. This is a very different activity, as you can see, from assuming that they've been demolished or "consciously raised" out of existence just because you've both agreed they ought to be. The hard fact is that sexism is here — if not to stay, then certainly for the long haul. You don't just make it disappear by deciding that the man should do the dishes or that the woman should be "on top."

What does this look like from a social therapeutic point of view? A man and a woman who want to be intimate with each other have to create their own man-woman relationship (a developmental zone). They need to break out of the sexist pattern which requires the woman to give as much as she can in order to get something from the man, while the man gives as little as possible and takes as much as he can get. And they must refuse to fit into the prefabricated form of feminist "correctness," where the new rules and roles of feminism just replace the old rules and roles of sexism. Even "good" categories are still categories. They're still limiting, they're still non-creative, they're still anti-developmental.

Just because women did X, Y and Z in the "bad old days" of sexism (which, of course, are to some extent still with us), it's a mistake to assume that everything will be great if they stop doing X, Y and Z and start doing A, B and C — even if "Do A, B and

C" is a "better" rule. So Jenny and Frank may decide that when they have sex she should "come first," but what if neither of them enjoys sex that way? The fact is that such a rule is no more "theirs" than the 10,000-year-old rule which says they should do it the opposite way. You see, simply negating something doesn't necessarily change anything. If you've lived your life consciously doing everything exactly the opposite of what, and how, your mother did things, you're as determined by Mom as those who say they are, and want to be, exactly like her.

It's simply not enough to have the "correct" insight, the "enlightened" morality, or even the "right" attitude. Men and women still have to build something growthful with that, and everything else that they bring to this activity (using all that they both are). Doing that together, sharing the responsibility for creating a new (their own) man-woman relationship, is profoundly intimate. It will look many different ways, depending on who the people are and what they want to create with one another.

Which brings us around, again, to why it's so hard to do. Well, there's the force of habit, which holds us back. But it's not only that. Both men and women have acquired real skills and strengths from doing the man-woman relationship in the old (oppressive) ways: men are often smarter, in the sense of being more worldly-wise; women, being less invested in how much they know, tend to be better at learning.

Speaking social therapeutically (which means not moralistically but from a developmental point of view), the issue is not whether to give up the old oppressive ways but *how* to give them up. How do you create something positive and new and developmental using skills and strengths that are a product of those old ways you're trying to get rid of? How do we rebuild the boat while we're sailing across the ocean on it? How do you create with feminism, rather than casting it in the role of a new authority figure (like The Church, The In-Laws, or The Neighbors) that dominates your relationship from outside?

What it takes is continuously reorganizing everything you have — especially the differences between men and women — and the difficulties that are raised for both of you by creating something new with what there is. The possibilities are endless, and endlessly exciting.

A good relationship, in my opinion, requires giving to the relationship what has been acquired (good and bad) in the old sexist arrangement. It involves consciously taking the radically uneven development of the old arrangement and giving it to a new and cooperative arrangement. This might lead to the two of you doing some things very differently from before, other things exactly like you did them before, and quite a few things simply other than before — including many things that you never did before.

The point is that we don't have to act out the roles of a sexist and getting culture that are so hurtful (to both women and men, and especially to women). In honestly recognizing sexism, with all its complex, uneven and unfair consequences, we can begin to reshape the totality of our relationship with someone of the "opposite" sex (not simply negate each particular element of it). We can thereby produce something — a new kind of relationship (a new totality) — of our own making.

EXERCISE:

Think of something the woman or man you're closest to does that you find irritating — the thing that makes you say: "Isn't that just like a woman!" or "Isn't that just like a man!" For one whole day practice being radically accepting of her or him, including the thing that irritates you.

5

Listening

I really like hearing what other people have to say. After nearly 60 years of listening, I still feel a sense of wonder at this remarkable activity called "speaking to each other" that we humans do together. I have a similar fascination with performance and the theatre; I've always been absolutely intrigued and entranced by what I see and hear on a stage. When I settle into my theatre seat, I'm not there as a critic — I'm not looking to judge whether the performance is "good" or "bad," or whether it's a work of "art" or not. I feel no need at all to judge it — still less to have someone else judge it for me. I'm just moved and delighted that people are up there performing, imitating, acting, putting on a show, creating something. I think it's wonderful, I appreciate it, and I clap like mad at the end.

And that's exactly how I feel about speaking. It's a performance, and I'm in the play. It's marvelous to me that people create meaning together, and no less marvelous for the fact that most of us take it completely for granted. So when I say that I really like listening, I'm not just talking about listening to certain people talk about certain subjects in a certain way — I mean that I like listening, period. I find speaking fascinating, regardless of what the speaker is saying (or how he or she is saying it).

Listening is the quintessential completing activity; it's what the other person or people (whoever is not speaking) has to do, or give, for communication to take place. By "completing," I'm not talking about finishing, or putting closure on, what someone has said, but about continuing the activity — initiated by the speaker — of communicating. If someone speaks but no one listens, the speaker (whether he or she is physically alone or not and regardless of his or her intentions) isn't communicating. Think of the exasperated father who says to his teenage son: "Talking to you is like talking to the wall!" or the hurt wife who says to her husband: "You haven't heard a word I've said!" or the irritated bus driver who says to a passenger: "I just told you that I don't go across town. Are you deaf?" What the speakers are expressing in these situations is their experience of not being completed, of not communicating. It's not "enough" that they're speaking; the people they're speaking to aren't listening. At this point in the non-dialogue, the father, the wife, and the driver may decide to start shouting, or swearing, or both — which makes it even more unlikely that the son, the husband and the passenger will be inclined to listen.

As with other social activities, there are many kinds of listening. Passively keeping your mouth closed while another person talks to you is very different from active listening. Just as people can play tennis more or less intensely, make love more or less passionately, and dance with more or less oomph, there's listening — and there's listening. It's possible to listen without really hearing, or to listen "with just half an ear." It's also possible to listen so closely and attentively that you do more than simply hear the words being said; you actually experience the other person as a whole human being engaged in the effort to communicate — to create — with language being the instrument, like a shared paint brush, for doing so.

Listening actively in this way is a kind of "performance." Active listeners show they're listening — they nod their heads; they smile; they express their surprise and their concern; they ask questions. They don't need to get anything from the speaker. They participate by hearing.

I think many people have a hard time listening. I'm not the only person to think so, by the way; for the last ten years or so, a number of major American corporations have been spending significant amounts of money on training their employees to listen. Of course, ordinary folks at home have been aware of the "communication gap" for a lot longer than that. I didn't discover that people don't listen to one another very well; the social therapeutic approach just has a cure (not a solution!) for it.

Why is listening so hard? In my opinion, it has to do with the inclination of many people to focus on particular products (meanings) rather than on the totality of the speaking activity (the qualitative process of creating meaning). Their listening is overdetermined by their need to know what the speaker is talking about. That someone is speaking is often related to as incidental at best, inconvenient or downright annoying at worst: "Get to the point!" they say impatiently to the speaker. "Spit it out!"

At these times, people are listening primarily so that when their own "turn" comes they'll be able to explain, interpret, make analogies or "identify" with what's been said by putting it into pre-existing, comprehensible categories. This way of relating to speaking — categorizing what's said according to what may or may not be "worth" listening to — is typically judgmental.

When language is overidentified with meaning, therefore, it stops being an instrument of communication and creation. It becomes, instead, a barrier to the understanding that comes from participating together in the joint activity of people speaking to each other. This can be enormously painful and frustrating, particularly when people are speaking of their emotional experiences. Yet this "language-overdetermined-by-meaning" often dominates traditional, so-called "insight-oriented" talk therapy, and the kinds of conversations between friends, family members and lovers that are modeled on it (or that it is modeled on).

Anthony is a junior in high school who told his guidance counselor that he doesn't want to go to college. When she responded "understandingly" that he was trying to "punish" his parents, Anthony stopped talking to her. He now reads a comic book whenever he's summoned to her office. The guidance counselor has complained to his parents that their 17-year-old son is "dumping" on her. According to her, Anthony is "at that stage where he has to confront the authority figures in his life and he's afraid of the emotional risks involved in doing that, especially with his mother." Her only "evidence" for this "analysis" is that Anthony's mother is the same age as the guidance counselor and is studying to be a guidance counselor herself!

You may think that this is an extreme example of judgmental, insight-oriented categorizing being substituted for the activity of listening. Unfortunately, in my experience, it's simply extremely common.

The trouble with such categorical and judgmental listening is that it doesn't allow those who are "listening" to hear much. They're so preoccupied with getting particular meanings that they miss, or dismiss, the totality of what the other person is saying. It's been my experience that when we don't listen "for" meaning in what other people say, we're much more likely to discover the person who's speaking — and whatever brilliance, wit, subtlety and charm that may be there.

In social therapy, we work to create an environment in which people can engage in the activity of listening to one another. We do that by challenging the meaning-dominated, "insight-oriented" categorical listening that's typical in a culture of getting. When one member of the group, A, speaks and another member of the group, B, responds judgmentally/categorically/insightfully, someone in the group is likely to tell B: "I don't think you heard what A said. Stop trying to get it. Instead, give something to the activity of speaking together."

Although I don't listen to people merely because I believe that it's morally correct to do so, there is a morality to that activity. As a practitioner of social therapy, I place a high value on people's efforts to create meaning through speaking. I think it is one of the principal ways in which we give expression to our humanity.

EXERCISE:

Here's a completing game that will help you to practice creating a listening environment.

Tell a collective story. Each person says one sentence, and no one can contradict what someone has said earlier. Example: The first person says, "I flew to the moon the other night." The next person says, "It took me much longer than usual, because of the accident." And so on.

6

Family Values

For the last hundred years or more, the institution of The Family has been analyzed by social scientists of every persuasion. Some of them, it seems to me, have had some valuable things to say on the subject.

There's all the difference in the world, of course, between a group of people who share a life together and consider themselves to be a family (your family, my family, whoever's family), and The Family (with a capital *F*), which as a societal institution exercises enormous influence over all of us (whether we live in a family or not). I think it's helpful to view the institution as both an ongoing play and a drama school.

Most people tend to act out family life according to the societal script "written" for roles in the play, "The Family" — Wife, Husband, Mother, Father, Daughter, Son, Sister and Brother — roles in which we have been cast primarily on the basis of age and gender. We are much less likely to "improvise" with the people who share our lives.

It is very typical, for example, for members of families to say things to each other like: "Don't talk to your father that way!" or "You're my wife...that's why you should come with me!"

The Family drama school is where we first learn that there are such things as roles, and we learn how to play them. The roles of Mother and Father require parents to teach their children how to act "right," which they do in many different ways. They go over and over the rules of good behavior: "Sit up straight." "Wash your hands before you eat." "Don't talk with your mouth full." "Say thank you." "Don't interrupt." They buy their children "appropriate" toys (trucks for boys, dolls for girls) to play with. And they act as role models that children imitate without ever being told to do so.

Like all acting parts, "Family" roles come with a fixed set of *do*s and *don't*s that govern everything from what, how and when everyone eats to where they sleep and with whom. Roles also come with a fixed set of values — the authoritative reasons that are invoked to justify the rules. You've probably heard them (or said them) a million times: "Because I said so." "Don't argue with your mother." "That's what the Bible (or Dr. Spock, or whoever) teaches us." "This is how we've always done it." "That's just good manners." "I'm trying to teach you some common sense."

Home is the theatre where "The Family" play runs, all day and all night long. It's also the "rehearsal" space where children are prepared for the roles they will assume as adults, when they'll be expected to have a family of their own. It's here that we first learn the limits of who we are, as societally defined: "Daddy's girl," "the baby of the family," "a troublemaker," "a brain," "a little gentleman," "a problem child." Ironically, we learn those roles so well that we come to think of playing them as "doing what comes naturally."

The notion that "real life" is "natural" and theatre is "artificial" seems just plain silly to me. After all, what's called "natural" is simply the acting out of predetermined roles in a play that was written long before any of us had anything to say about it. As I see it, the only way we can actually create who we are in this kind of societal environment is to perform.

Imagine drawing a chalk circle and then saying to your child, your mother-in-law, or your co-worker: "I don't think that last half hour of life was very good. Let's step over onto that stage and perform it differently." Why should performance only take place in special places called "theatres" where specially trained "actors" do their thing?

For the last ten years I've been working, as a playwright and a director, with a number of very talented people to create what I call developmental theatre. I'd be delighted to have you come and see one of our plays at the Castillo Theatre in Manhattan the next time you're in New York.

At Castillo we are creating theatre that's not overdetermined by the preconceptions of the playwright, the director, the critics, the audience or anyone else. The trouble with having a fixed, idealized vision of what a play ought to be is that the ideal is constantly "telling" you whether you're doing it "right" or "wrong." It doesn't allow you to take everything — "good" and "bad" — and do something developmental with it.

So we take all of the elements available to us — the script; the talents, personalities, looks and experiences of the actors; the skills and ideas of the "technical" crew; old plays (our own and others), which we rework and combine — and create with all of it. We're constantly playing around with the elements that we have, to see how they can be used to "complete" each other in the creation of a performance. Rather than making a theatre piece conform to a preconceived plan so that we end up with a product we had in mind all along, we engage in a developmental process and see what comes of it.

That is, as well, the social therapeutic approach to life: we help people to create their lives continuously, out of whatever there is. We teach them to "do" life as a developmental theatre performance. (Twice a year I conduct weekend workshops where large groups of people — some of them social therapy patients and some not — practice this activity by producing and performing a play that we create then and there.)

As family members, co-workers, friends and lovers, none of us has to act out the roles in which we've been cast. No one has to know beforehand how the "play" is going to turn out. All of us can perform our lives — and if we don't like how it goes, we can do a different performance the next day, the next hour, or the next minute! Completing, not competing, is the way to do it.

What it means to complete is to respond to whatever happens as something that could transform the totality of what's going on. Someone does something different, something new, something unexpected — and now the whole thing is different and new! Your play may have started out as a murder mystery, but it could turn out to be a musical comedy, science fiction, a quiz show or — who knows what? It doesn't have to be the realization of a preconceived plan.

One thing that keeps people from completing rather than competing is the tendency to assume that a story has to go a certain way. Most people tend to think that if you start out with A, B and C, then you have to do D, E and F — regardless of how you and the other performers responded to A, B and C. In other words, they tend to think that how the story was preconceived has to determine how it will turn out. And then they compete to see who can come up with the right ending.

But just because you've gone to a football game doesn't mean that you have to stay until the end of the last quarter. Just because you're in bed with someone doesn't mean that you have to have sex. Nor does it mean that, if you do have sex, it has to go a certain way. Just because you have a degree in accounting doesn't mean that you can't decide to become a nurse, an artist, or anything else…

Maybe there is no "right" ending. This is what the social therapeutic approach helps people to see: as human beings, we can create something new from whatever there is.

In doing therapy with members of a family, the social therapeutic task is to create an environment where we can expose how heavily societal roles press down on everyone in it, and how "The Family" itself — as the play — forces them to stay locked into those roles. When families come to me for help, I ask everyone: "Who here is ready to participate in the work of creating what this group of people is and redefining what you can do together? Who is going to stand up for all of you, and not just for this or that role? Who is willing to put aside the 'The Family' script so that you can create something together that allows all of you to grow and to develop?"

In other words, the social therapeutic approach helps people to determine what they want their family to be; it's not about coaching them to say their lines in the script better, or getting them to adjust to the roles they've been given so that they can put on a better act.

Take Dorothy and her family. At 70, Dorothy is having an extended temper tantrum. She stays at home all day, sleeping and watching television. At nights and on weekends she refuses to go anywhere with her husband, Norman, a successful businessman who at 71 loves going out. Dorothy is always angry at someone: Norman, for something he said or did half a century ago; her daughter, for getting divorced; her daughter-in-law, for the "inconsiderate" way she treats Dorothy; lifelong friends, for not inviting her to something; the cleaning lady, for coming too late, or too early.

Although her doctor says she's in excellent health, Dorothy tells her family that she "knows" she's dying. When her daughter urges her to "get out," Dorothy smiles sadly and says that no one understands how it feels to be "old and fat and ugly."

I believe very strongly that the most respectful and loving thing you can do with people, including old people, is to make the demand that they continue to grow. What I mean by this is to demand that they participate with you in the lifelong process of reshaping and reorganizing what your family is — to make it an environment where everyone in the family, young and old, women and men, is supported to develop. Anything else — compelling them to remain in the roles of Mother and Father, or reversing the roles and becoming their Parent — is deadening for everyone concerned.

Terrific! you may say. *But that seems terribly hard to do.* It is! All of us, including old people themselves, have been taught that the elderly have nothing left to give, emotionally, intellectually, or otherwise. They're typically viewed, and view themselves, as victims — of time, circumstance, poor health, their children, or all of the above. Chances are that they're ill, or unable to see, or hear, or walk very well. They may be in pain or unable to think very clearly. Like Dorothy, they may be grieving over a "loss" (in her case, her youth) that can never be "made good." From a societal point of view, they — and those who care for them — may ask: "Why bother?"

So we hesitate to tell them that they need to continue to grow. And they're likely to insist that they can't and won't. That, in my opinion, is the real reason why so many old people often feel humiliated, bored, sad, angry and exhausted. So do five-year-olds, 15-year-olds, 45-year-olds, and other human beings who are forced to exist in no-growth environments.

Oh! you may be thinking. *I get it. You're talking about encouraging old folks to take an interest, to get off their duffs...* No. Encouragement is often a polite form — if there is such a thing — of coercion: getting other people to do what you want them to do, or think they ought to do, "for their own good." The environment I'm talking about doesn't have an end in sight and it's not overdetermined by judgments. This kind of environment is characterized by radical acceptance.

How do you make the demand, in practice, that old people develop? You do it by imitating how adults relate to very young children when they're first learning to speak. Create an environment in which you support them to do what they don't know how to do, and accept whatever it is that they do. That's the developmental activity which enables children to grow, and it works for grownups too — if they choose to participate.

From the social therapeutic point of view, every human being — whatever his or her psychological "diagnosis," score on a standard "IQ" test, "age," or any other societal label — has an unlimited capacity for development. Accordingly, the social therapeutic approach relates to people not in terms of their "pathology" or their "problems," but as human beings who may be undeveloped, or underdeveloped, but whose development can nevertheless be reinitiated at any time. The capacity for development is what makes us human. From this point of view, to relate to people non-developmentally — regardless of their age, or anything else — is therefore inhuman.

EXERCISE:

This can help you and the people you live with to "take an intermission" from "The Family" play and see it from another vantage point.

Ask someone in your family to exchange roles with you for a day.

7

Kid Stuff

Playing a role — whether you're the star or a walk-on, Lady Macbeth or her Lady-in-Waiting — can be very limiting. Think of all the things you have to do and say just because you're "The Child," and all the things you're not allowed to do or say just because you're "The Mother."

Things are even more complicated these days, when our culture is changing very rapidly. Many of us aren't even sure what "role" we're in. It might have changed since last year, last month, last week — yesterday!

Consequently, nowadays children are often more worldly-wise than their parents. Youngsters of nine and ten are likely to understand how fast things are changing — after all, they were born into this rapidly changing world. Meanwhile, their Moms and Dads may still think that things are changing at the rate they were changing 25 years ago, when they were young. Chances are that Mom and Dad are "out of step," unhip to the quantitative and the qualitative character of change these days.

A few years ago I spoke about this with a group of middle-aged working women taking an introductory psychology course taught by a colleague of mine in a trade union college program. Many of them told me they were enormously relieved. They had thought there was something terribly wrong with them for feeling that their kids knew more than they did.

The fact is that there's a built-in contradiction between what the traditional societal role of Parent (with a capital P) requires adults to do and the new societal reality. The traditional requirement is that adults help children adapt to the world. The new reality is that today's children are often better qualified to help adults adapt to the world.

Typically, children understand this and adults don't. Or adults refuse to acknowledge it, which comes down to the same thing. It's a major source of conflict in many, many families. Parents may have societal (legal, religious and moral) authority, but they aren't very capable of making anything happen. A lot of energy is devoted to promoting the cultural myth that "Father (or Mother) Knows Best," but kids know that they often don't. What's worse, many parents don't even know they don't know.

This situation is very different, by the way, from the typical experience of the immigrant family in America. In that family, it's always been legitimate and "perfectly natural" for children learning to be Americans in school and on the streets to say to their parents: "You don't understand this new country, its currency, or its customs. You don't speak its language. I'll show you how to get along, and I'll even do the talking for you." As newcomers to America who couldn't be expected to know the ropes, immigrant parents have been able to hear and accept that statement as a matter of fact, with nothing very shameful about it.

But what contemporary children are saying to their "born in the USA" parents is neither "natural" nor "acceptable." It goes like this: "The very fact that you've adapted yourself to this society for the last 35 years makes it practically impossible for you to know what's really going on, which is that society itself is transforming with extraordinary rapidity and in ways you don't even know about. Most of what you 'know,' including how you know how to learn, is obsolete and irrelevant. Moms, Pops — you don't dig the haps!"

Teachers face the same dilemma that parents do. They too are cast in roles that were "written" for the world as it was, yet they're supposed to teach kids how the world is. They often don't know any better than parents do. But, like parents, they're expected to act as if they've got it all together.

It's as if parents and teachers had learned to swim in a small, shallow backyard pool. Now they suddenly find themselves in the middle of the ocean — and they're trying to tell a youngster who's been in the ocean for the last eight or 10 or 14 years how to swim. The "swimming pool experts," in adapting themselves to the swimming pool, have allowed themselves to be formed (actually, *deformed*) by that environment. Their very expertise places limits on their continued growth, especially under changed conditions. From the social therapeutic perspective, they are underdeveloped. If they're going to learn something new, they've got to unlearn much of what they know. This is something which many people do not do easily or well in our culture of getting, because they're committed to holding on to what they've got.

Children born in the ocean, however, are simply undeveloped. They haven't been miseducated yet, so all they have to do is learn what they don't know. They tend to be good learners because they have no investment in pretending to know what they don't know.

I'm not seeking to glorify children, or to put down parents. The point I'm making is that our rapidly changing world demands a new approach to learning and development.

In doing therapy with parents, I try to help them see that they have to decide on a child-rearing *strategy*. There are at least two choices. One is to maximize whatever immediate gratification an adult may get as the mother or father of a child — what makes the family look good, or maybe even what makes the parents feel good. The other is for the adult to do whatever he or she can to enhance the likelihood that this young person will be able to live in the world when he or she is no longer a child — a hard thing to do, given the rate at which our world is changing.

Why do parents have to make this choice? Because these two strategies aren't compatible. The first has to do with Mom and Dad getting something for themselves, although it's almost always expressed as being "for the good of the children." The second has to do with Mom and Dad giving what they've got to the grown-ups their children will someday be.

What the first strategy looks like is that you, the parent, reward and punish your children to get them to say and do the right thing for the moment: making their beds, minding their manners, making the team, playing the piano, earning good grades, having nice friends. According to this strategy, your kids are responsible for helping you to show the world — your in-laws, your neighbors, and anyone else who might be watching — that this family is putting on an Academy Award-winning version of "The Family."

The second strategy requires that as a parent you work with your children to create what this thing called "childhood" is so that they have the tools they'll need to create and live their lives later on. It does not come, as the first one does, with a script; this is a play you create in performing it. It's improvisational.

Now the immediate consequences of pursuing this strategy may be less immediately gratifying and attractive than what the first one yields. Maybe your children won't act right when they get to their grandmother's house — or maybe they won't want to go at all. They might not want to go to church or to school, either. In saying this, I'm not advocating an "anything goes" policy, or suggesting that the kids should "run the show." I am saying that if you choose to create a life with your children based on the strategic perspective of giving what you have to them rather than getting what you can from them, then you run certain risks that parents who choose the getting strategy don't have to face.

One consequence of having a strategic perspective on child rearing is that it shapes your responses to situations as they occur, hour to hour, day to day. When something goes "wrong," for example, the first strategy leads you to say: This looks bad! It generates questions like: How can we make sure this never happens again — or at least that it doesn't happen tomorrow? The second strategy produces statements like: Forget how it looks! And it yields questions like: How can we build on it? How can what has happened contribute to the developmental process, to a learning that leads development? This is the kind of learning that's "in advance of" what someone is able to do at a given moment — like the learning that takes place in very early childhood, when adults relate to babies and young children as speakers before the little ones "know" how to talk.

To ask the second kind of question, you have to be very open to learning and doing new things — particularly to learning new things from and doing new things with your children. But it isn't easy when you're locked into the traditional parent role, which requires you to act as if you know more, and "better," than they do.

Mary Ann is a single mother whose nine-year-old son, Mike, refuses to go to school this year. He's pretty clear about his reasons, too. He says that his class is "the worst" in the school (which uses a tracking system), and that everyone — the principal, the teachers, and the other kids — treat the children in 4C "like we're dummies." Mike says he isn't learning anything in school this year, and that his teacher is "mean."

Mary Ann is determined to play out this scenario in a traditional way. In a social therapy session, she acknowledges that, so far as she can tell, everything Mike says is true — "but it doesn't matter." Mary Ann's position is that, when it comes to her son, she knows it all: "He has to go, whether he likes it or not," she tells me. "That's life, and the sooner he finds it out, the better."

But although she's tried everything to get him to go to school — threats, promises, "reasoning" with him — when morning comes, Mike turns his face to the wall and won't get out of bed. Like many parents, Mary Ann has painted herself into a corner. The more she insists on her identity as a knower ("I'm the mother here. I'm the adult. I know what's best for you"), the less able she is to give Mike what she knows that could be helpful to a nine-year-old boy in a difficult situation. ("Let's try to figure this thing out together.")

This is what the social therapeutic approach helps parents to do: to learn how to learn from their children so that they, the adults, can shape and give direction to what the young people know about the world as it is now.

Many years ago, when my daughter Elizabeth (now in her early thirties) was very young, I decided that I wanted to be available to her after she grew up, to be someone she could turn to. I didn't want to get stuck in the position of always telling her what to do then, to "overplay" my hand (my role) as her father. My concern was what her life — including our relationship — would look like when she was an adult. How would it be, look and feel 20 years and 30 years down the road?

I had been the youngest of five children; the brother who was closest to me in age was seven years older and my other brothers were in their late teens when I was born. My sister, who brought me up, was 16 years older than I was. The childrearing "policy," where I was concerned, was something like "benign neglect."

By the time I was a father myself, I realized that this was not the worst thing that could have happened to me. It seemed to me that my friends whose mothers had watched over them, worried excessively about them, and waited on them with such intensity had not benefited very much from all that undoubtedly well-meant attention. Although I had not been particularly supported to develop, no one ever "sat on" me, either. I had managed to grow up, and was living my life. At the very least, I wanted that for my daughter. I also wanted her to be able to have me in her life if she wanted me and how she wanted me.

A word or two about wanting and needing. From a social therapeutic point of view, wanting is much more about giving; needing tends to be more about getting. To be wanting of someone has to do with who that person is. What it means to be wanted is to be known, and to be given to. Needing usually has more to do with who the needer is, and what the person who is needed has to give.

Now I don't think it's terrible, or unhealthy, or a "bad sign" of anything when people need each other. In our culture, probably most relationships — including very caring and intimate ones — are characterized by both wanting and needing. I do think that it's healthier when wanting-giving is the "senior partner" in our closest relationships, and less healthy when needing-getting takes precedence.

One day, during the summer that my daughter was eight, she and I were walking on the beach in eastern Long Island. Elizabeth was skipping along at the edge of the water, occasionally running in a little way to meet a wave. Although she was in no danger, I wanted to warn her about the undertow. I wanted to stop her — and then I realized that this eight-year-old didn't have to be afraid of what I, a 33-year-old man at the time, was afraid of. The rules had to be based on what *she* needed to be safe, not on *my* need as a parent to "know" that she was safe. I wanted her to lead her life, not mine.

I let Elizabeth know that I was there for her, but that I didn't need to determine her life. I didn't particularly "need" her at all. I didn't spend all those years of her childhood worrying about her.

Now that she's grown up, she's not spending all these years worrying about me. I want her as much as I always did, and I love being wanted by her.

Although Elizabeth is my biological child, I'm not her Father and she's not my Daughter. We've chosen to create our own relationship rather than to "have" the ready-made one that gets handed down to fathers and daughters in our culture. One consequence of that choice is that I haven't always known what I was doing, and neither has she. We didn't have rules to go by beforehand; we've created them in the process of building our relationship. So there were times — especially when Elizabeth was young — when I didn't "look good" (that is, like a "responsible father") to those members of our family who wanted us to look much more like a Family (with a capital *F*). But over the years she and I have managed to create something that's of real value to both of us.

Now if you've ever been a parent, or a child (I guess that means all of us!), you'll understand that I made mistakes in my relationship with Elizabeth. I can think of 1,001 things I could have done differently — and better. The social therapeutic approach is not any sort of guarantee against making mistakes. The point I'm making here is that, as a parent, I wasn't trying to get it right — and I didn't demand that my daughter get it right. That has made it possible for us to be radically accepting of one another. You're no less your child's parent for being her friend — or for not knowing how to do it.

EXERCISE:

Here's a good way for any adult (not just parents) to practice not being a know-it-all.

Ask a child to teach you how to do something you don't know how to do.

8

Guilt, Shame, and Your 'My-ness'

Most of us have a belief system, a point of view, that is likely to include moral and ethical principles and/or religious values. I am deeply committed to the position that everyone on earth should have the right to freedom of religion and freedom of thought. But ethical and religious views are not the same as a science of human growth and development.

Take Freudian psychology, a make-believe science based on a secularized view of religion.

Freud characterized the human mind as a moral battleground, where the supernatural ("subconscious") forces of good (the "superego") and evil (the "id") struggle for possession of the human soul (the "ego"). Obviously, he was borrowing heavily from Jewish and Christian Scriptures. He took the tapestry of Western religion and shaped an abnormal psychology in its image. No wonder Freudian psychology has been offending believers in science, believers in religion, and people who are both, ever since.

Having pseudo-religiously "established" the nature of the mind, Freud concluded — pseudo-scientifically — that the world was a reflection of it. To Freudians, the world is the way it is because the minds of individuals make it that way.

Let's take a look at how traditional Freudian-influenced psychology understands guilt. In most forms of Christianity and Judaism, guilt plays a major role. So it's not surprising that in traditional psychology guilt is the primary emotion — but with an anti-religious and unscientific twist. While religion views guilt as an objective inner sign that corresponds to the wrongdoing of someone who knows the difference between "right" and "wrong," psychology views guilt as an emotion attached to wrong desires that have supposedly been with us from our earliest years — when, presumably, little boys want to kill their daddies so they can have sex with their mommies, and little girls decide that since they can't have penises, they'll have babies instead.

In contrast to traditional psychology, the social therapeutic approach doesn't view guilt as an emotion at all. Rather, I think that guilt is best understood as a way of believing — judgmentalism. It's deeply rooted in the Judeo-Christian religious worldview, which involves the "recognition" of wrongdoing as judged by the criteria of a moral and religious universe.

From the social therapeutic point of view, the primary emotional experience in our culture is not guilt, but shame. People very often do feel ashamed or humiliated. I believe that shame has to do with how we feel about our bodies and our lives and our consequent efforts to keep certain things (both physical and emotional) hidden from view.

You might say that guilt is how human beings relate cognitively and morally to our Gods, while shame has more to do with how we relate to other human beings. Shame is a measure of our distance from one another. From this point of view, intimacy is — among other things — the sharing of our shame, our humiliation, with other people; it is an ongoing exposing to them of all that we are, physically and emotionally.

In our culture, shame is typically "covered over" by other emotions. It's the emotion that's most often "repressed." When people get angry, for example, they're often "repressing" their humiliation, which they feel too ashamed to express directly. Being disappointed or scared, losing your way, not having the answer, the money, or the right clothes...all are occasions for feeling ashamed in a culture of getting, where everyone is expected to "have it all together," to "be with it" and to "act cool." It's easier for most people to be angry with themselves and other people than to say: "I feel humiliated. I feel mortified. I feel ashamed."

The social therapeutic approach to dealing with the pseudo-emotion of guilt is to teach people how to create environments where making judgments is not the dominant activity. The significance of guilt as an "emotional" factor is thereby reduced. Within these relatively judgment-free — and therefore relatively guilt-free — environments, the conditions exist for dealing more constructively with shame.

The social therapy group is one such environment. A group of friends, members of a family, and lovers can also work to build their relationships as judgment-free, guilt-free "zones." This is not to say that no one will ever have judgments in those environments; rather, judgmentalism is not the dominant activity in them.

How do you deal constructively with shame? We do it in social therapy groups (and you can do it wherever you have created such an environment) by breaking down, or deconstructing, people's isolated, privatized, possessive notions of the self — what I call "my-ness." Because it's only when you hold on to an excessively individualistic identity that you can have something to be ashamed of: how you did in bed last night; what you look like in a bathing suit; the dumb thing you said to your best friend's husband; the fight you had with your seven-year-old son; the other fight you had with your 77-year-old mother; getting a little drunk after you lost the game, and losing your temper...

You're only vulnerable to feeling humiliated (and then covering up the humiliation) to the extent that you're invested in your identity as a good lover, a good looker, a good friend, a good mother, a good daughter, a good sport.

The social therapeutic approach challenges "my-ness" by creating environments in which people can practice a cultural alternative to the private possession of human commodities — including our selves — that characterizes our highly competitive culture of getting.

Completion is the name we've given to the life activity that is the cultural alternative to competition. It's an activity in which nearly all human beings participate as very young children. When babies first begin to speak, older children and adults "complete" for them: the baby (an "inexperienced" speaker) makes some sounds — "Ba...ba..." — and the older child or the adult (an "experienced" speaker) says: "Bottle? You want your bottle! You're thirsty after your nap, aren't you?" As adults, we typically don't compete with babies. We don't tell them what *we* want, or whether *we're* thirsty, or what *we* prefer to drink when we wake up. We don't wait for babies to stop making sounds so that we can take our turn in the conversation, as we often do with other adults.

Such an environment, where completing is the dominant activity, is relatively free of judgments, and therefore of guilt. The baby isn't being judged on its competence as a speaker — there's no question of guilt because, in this environment, there's no "right" and "wrong," "good" and "bad." Rather than making judgments, the adult is practicing radical acceptance — whatever the baby says is whatever the baby says.

Such an environment is often relatively shame-less as well. In the profoundly intimate, profoundly social activity of completing and working together ("conjointly" is the technical term some of my academic colleagues use), "my-ness" is as absent as judgments. The baby knows no shame because he or she doesn't have anything to hide; babies have no identity, as "good" speakers or anything else. Very young children aren't afraid to explore who they are. They haven't come up with an identity yet. So nothing they do is humiliating to them. One human being, the baby, shows and gives what he or she can do to another human being, the adult. That other human being doesn't compete with but completes for the first. They create something new together out of what they each bring to this joint activity.

As you can probably tell, the "environment" in which we first learn to speak isn't a place, but a complex social activity. Very young children are supported to go "beyond themselves" by doing what they don't know how to do — and they do! In a remarkably short time (long before they know the rules of grammar, or even that there are such things), these newcomers to human society are not only asking for their juice, but singing songs, making up jokes, and telling stories — all in a language they've made their own and, at the same time, have begun to give something new to.

Learning to speak is a striking example of the completely ordinary miracle of human development. If babies and little children weren't related to in this way — if they weren't supported to learn "in advance of" their development — there'd be no accounting for development at all. Even more importantly, there wouldn't *be* any development; we'd all still be talking baby talk and crawling around the living room. Completion is what makes it possible for us to grow.

Of course, conventional learning — acquiring information that can be inserted into the formulas, patterns and categories we already know — is profoundly useful when you're trying to build a bridge or put out a fire. But when we allow this quantitative, acquisitive and competitive learning model to dominate, or define, what learning is, we do so at the expense of the coming-into-being, creative dimension of life — the unique and unlimited capacity to develop that makes us human.

The social therapeutic approach teaches people to create environments where the developmental activity of completing takes precedence over role-determined, rule-governed competitive behavior. How? By playing language games. That is, we actively challenge competitive culture as it's expressed in language — most particularly the language that's used to talk about emotions, desires and intentions. And at the same time we use the very "stuff" left lying around by that deconstructive activity of breaking down language to create something new — new meanings and a new language, new emotions and a new emotionality.

We've all been taught to assume that the meaning of what we say lies in the content of our words, rather than in the activity of our saying them. The social therapeutic approach teaches people to play language games as an antidote to the Explanatory, Interpretive, Insightful method which traditional, Freudian-influenced clinical psychology uses to drag "hidden meanings" from the depths of the speaker's "subconscious." Here's how you play.

"I made a commitment to talking more," Paula tells her social therapy group one evening. As the therapist, I take this statement as an invitation to play a language game. I ask the group — including Paula — what she is doing when she says "I made a commitment to talking more."

In examining Paula's statement, it becomes clear that it's meant to make us — including Paula — think that her words correspond to or represent or reflect her desire to do something different: to participate more, to be more giving. But in saying these words, Paula's not doing anything very different; talking (a very little bit) about "talking more" is not the same as talking more. Indeed, if she were talking more, it wouldn't be necessary to say that she had "made a commitment" to doing so. Just imagine how odd it would be — not to mention dangerous — if, instead of breathing, people went around saying that they had "made a commitment" to breathing and then expected the rest of us to congratulate them for deciding to do the psychologically and physiologically right thing!

In saying "I made a commitment to talking more," Paula is doing what she usually does — which is to give as little as possible in order to get something for herself. In this case, what she's trying to get is the admiration and approval of the group. In playing the game of discovering what Paula was doing in saying what she said, rather than trying to interpret the "meaning" of it, I was taking what she said seriously. Responding to people in this way helps to create an environment in which the group can focus on activity rather than on abstract meanings.

The social therapy group is a child-like environment in that completing, not competing, is the dominant activity. You can create such an environment with the members of your household, or a group of friends, by getting rid of excessive "my-ness." What does this "my-ness" look like? Well, for example, when most people express an opinion, they don't merely say what they think — they convey that they're right: "I think we should keep the windows open." "I think the blue lamp would look better over there." "I think we should get a dog." "I think we should save the money and do it ourselves." "I think she needs to see a doctor." "I think that's the worst movie I've ever seen."

Why is it so necessary to be right? Because it's *my* opinion — what *I* think — and not merely an opinion. The possibility that my opinion might be wrong or mistaken — even the possibility that it might be seen as not being absolutely right — is humiliating to many people. Maybe the windows should be kept partly open. Maybe the blue lamp looks as good over here as over there. Maybe we should get a cat, too, or a turtle. Maybe we can get it done cheaply. Maybe all she needs is a good night's sleep. Maybe the movie wasn't all that bad.

People tend to be concerned about the prospect that their privately possessed beliefs could be wrong. It's humiliating to be wrong, so they hide behind their rightness. Not to be right is to be exposed as fallible, an ordinary human being capable — like everybody else — of making mistakes.

But in an environment where an opinion is merely an opinion, not a validation of "my-ness" (that is, my identity), there's not much room for humiliation. In these more child-like environments, we can grow more easily. When we teach each other to talk — when we complete each other — we're less likely to use words to compete with each other.

EXERCISES:

These can help you see what life is like on the other side of the "my-ness" fence.

1.   Say: "Oh! I'm wrong!" to someone you disagree with.

2.   Spend the day expressing other people's opinions instead of your own.

9

Sex and Friendship

In our culture, a lot of people are miserable because they just aren't any good at the getting game. Traditional psychology tends to view this as a "problem" that's somehow located in the individual "losers," who are diagnosed (or self-diagnosed) as deficient in the traits which supposedly make up the "well-adjusted" personality.

A case in point: the brand-new fourth edition of the American Psychiatric Association's *Diagnostic and Statistical Manual of Mental Disorders,* as pseudo-scientific a publication as you will ever come across, identifies something called "gender identity disorder" in children. One of the criteria for diagnosing this "illness" in boys is "an aversion to rough-and-tumble play with other boys, and a rejection of boys' typical toys, games and activities" — which characteristically reward aggression and competition.

From the perspective of traditional psychology — including most "pop" psychology — the "solution" to the "problem" is to make up the deficiency. Indeed, "making up for deficiencies" is the methodology of one of America's booming postmodern industries, the "quickie course."

The Learning Annex in New York City, which is geared to a market made up primarily of people in their twenties and thirties who want to improve their careers or their personal lives, offers hundreds of lectures and short courses ostensibly designed to teach them how to do it. The "problem," of course, does not lie in people's desire to have a better life, but in the cynical pseudo-solutions of most "quickie courses."

Not surprisingly, women — whose centuries-long societal training has virtually guaranteed that they would be losers in the getting game — are often the major targets when those non-solutions are advertised. Here are some course descriptions from a recent catalog put out by the Learning Annex.

"Be a Better Bitch — Does it bother you to be a nice, soft-hearted, good-natured person while getting little in return? You might be suffering from DMS (Doormat Syndrome). If you are, [the instructor] will show you it's time to wake up to reality and learn how to put your own needs first…Learn why bitches attract the best men — and why better bitches keep them!"

"How to Get Vengeance, Revenge and More — …you can learn how to make your target regret the day he (or she) was born, using totally legal and socially acceptable methods of revenge…"

"Steal the Man You Want From the Arms of Another Woman…or Just Keep the Man You Love — There's nothing more exciting than a well-manipulated man."

From the social therapeutic perspective, however, learning to "be a better bitch," to "make your target regret the day he (or she) was born," or to "steal the man you want" is not simply morally questionable. It's also highly unlikely to produce a more gratifying, more satisfying or fulfilling personal life! Now it's certainly true that some people can do all kinds of rotten things to other people and seem to have a ball doing it, while very nice people might spend a good deal of time feeling sad. However, in a quarter of a century of doing therapy, it's been my experience that people who are good at the getting game are often at least as miserable — alienated, deprived, self-degraded and emotionally un-nourished — as those who are bad at it.

In saying this, I want to make clear that I am not invoking the authority of morality, or anything else. As you've probably seen by now, the cultural experience of social therapy is informed by a moral principle which is very different from the one associated with the culture of getting. But I am speaking here from a scientific vantage point about a way of relating emotionally to other human beings (getting all you can) that, at this moment in the life and times of our species, is no longer conducive to the growth and development of individuals personally, or of our species. That's why so many people experience "the getting life" as destructive and self-destructive. It is.

You can see this very clearly in how most people conduct their sex lives, regardless of whether what they are doing is called "heterosexuality" or "homosexuality." Traditional sex — what I call attraction-based sex — as it is typically practiced in our culture of getting is male in its orientation (even for women).

What I am saying is that attraction and sex are closely connected to humiliation, the model of which is the humiliation of women. Much of sex, both heterosexual and homosexual, is designed to be humiliating.

Now I know you may find this shocking. Listen for a moment and try to be honest with yourself.

Humiliation is typically the turn-on, for women as well as for men. Think of all the movies which feature this kind of sex — such movies both influence and are influenced by normal sexual practices in America. Advertising, it seems to me, illustrates the sexual turn-on of humiliation very clearly. In saying this, I'm not suggesting that most men consciously seek to humiliate women (although, to be sure, some do). Nor am I suggesting that most women consciously seek to humiliate themselves or other women in order to be turned on (although some do become "better bitches").

Rather, the humiliation of women (like humiliation in general) in our culture acts in a more "subtle" and "normal" way as an aphrodisiac to stimulate ordinary, day in and day out sexual excitement. It's what sex *is* in our culture. Men — not "sickos," but ordinary, respectable, "nice" guys — fantasize about women "giving in," down on their knees, "asking for it." Women — not "weirdos," but ordinary, decent, caring women — often take pride in and are excited by knowing they've defeated other women on the battlefield of sex. Aggression and humiliation are what turn us on.

Again, put your moral judgments about this to the side for a moment and simply have a look at the movies, advertisements, TV shows, "pop" preachers and "private" fantasies. When I hear stories about the sex lives of men like Jimmy Swaggart and Jim Bakker, I'm not surprised. And I don't think Jimmy, Jim and Company are distinguishable from the millions who have followed them. Quite the contrary. It shows how come Jimmy and Jim are so in tune with their followers; it shows that when it comes to sexual matters, they really do have their fingers (or whatever) on the pulse (or whatever) of America.

Sexual attraction tends to be overdetermined by things that are, to some extent, out of our control: mass culture, physical appearance, stylized gestures and movements that are societally defined as desirable. Just look up at those billboards! Built into our cultural notions of attractiveness is a requirement of distance — it's how someone looks at arm's length, not real close up where physical characteristics become more of a blur. (Professional photographers know exactly what distance to be from the model to make her or him look the sexiest.)

In a getting culture, being "attracted" to someone initially — from a proper distance — typically implies that you "go and get it," or at least try. For a while, the getting (the seduction, the conquest, and the accompanying humiliation) is exciting. After that wears off, something else is usually required to "justify" or rationalize continuing to have sex: being "in love," getting married, having a baby, staying together "for the sake of the children." Is this picture true for everyone? Obviously not. On the other hand, we're not talking here about "deviant" behavior. For many people in our society, the sexual attraction (and everything that goes along with it) comes first; the friendship comes later, if at all.

This kind of sex — the standard sex that we have on the basis of attraction — tends to be primarily about conquest and domination, even for the one who's dominated. As societally organized aggression that's based on the mortification of one person by another, it's often brutal — not necessarily in its content (loving words and sincere intentions may accompany it) but in its form. Millions upon millions of tiny acts of domination and humiliation are experienced emotionally, even if they are not always understood intellectually, as such. That's a lot of what sex is in America (and elsewhere) nowadays.

In this kind of arrangement, "naturally," women are much more likely to be the ones who are hurt. But this is not to say that women are naturally more giving. On the contrary, women in our culture of getting are brought up to give their sexuality, their emotionality, their "understanding," and everything else only in order to get — and to value themselves accordingly. Most women are just not as good at getting as men are trained to be. This is one reason, in my opinion, that women often get so angry at men. Unlike Sigmund Freud, I don't believe that women are motivated primarily by "penis envy." I do think, however, that in the context of the culture of getting, they are quite justifiably envious — not of men's biological attributes, but of their superior societal endowments.

For the last 25 years, feminism has succeeded in helping some women to obtain "better terms" for their labors of love and, to some extent, for their work outside the home. These women may exercise some economic independence; their husbands may "help" with the housework and the child care. All of this, in my opinion, is great. But like a trade union which succeeds in negotiating an agreement with management that makes the job more bearable (shorter hours, improved working conditions, added benefits), workers are always vulnerable to losing whatever reforms they've won. As long as the getting activity remains fundamental in our emotional lives, women will remain sexually and personally humiliated objects of aggression. And men, as the humiliators in the conjoint "getting act," will experience less and less genuine intimacy.

In social therapy we help men and women to do sex quite differently. I sometimes, playfully, call this activity *friendosexuality*. It's a game that everyone — women and men, gay people and straight people — can play.

Friendosexuality means playing the sex game with a good friend instead of engaging in getting behavior with someone who is, effectively, a stranger (even if you've been sharing the same bed, and the same name, for the last 15 years).

The way that very young children play is the model for friendosexuality. Three-year-olds and four-year-olds create contexts for playing with their friends in which what they do — like rolling a ball back and forth to each other or spilling sand on one another — isn't guiltily perceived, morally overdetermined, or rooted in humiliation. It's not overloaded with interpretations. It's simply pleasurable and fun. I'm not advocating that adults do *what* children do, sexually or otherwise. Rather, the social therapeutic approach helps people do sex *how* the youngest children do playing.

Doing consensual sex with a friend is doing sex with a peer, an equal, rather than with someone who effectively exercises power over you or who defers to you. Such a sexual relationship, between equals, is not overdetermined by humiliation (or, in any event, the imposition of humiliation from the outside). In that kind of relationship, you can create your own turn-ons together.

Since we've all been socialized — by the movies, advertising, TV and the rest — to be turned on by humiliation, most people tend not to be very aware of what excites them. Deciding, consciously, what turns you on — even if what that is turns out to be relatively traditional and, perhaps, humiliating ways of doing sex (with the man on top, eyes closed and the lights out) — immediately transforms what you're doing sexually. As with so many other life activities, it's not the what of it that makes sex what it is, but the how. It's not as if certain sexual positions, kinds of underwear or words are or are not humiliating in and of themselves; no small part of what makes them what they are is how they're used, and who's deciding to use them.

What's the alternative to the attraction-humiliation organization of sex that's so commonplace in our culture of getting? It's building an environment in which people who are doing sex together can be giving to each other, and can support one another to be giving to other people. In other words, it's creating a friendship.

What I mean by friendship is not something that people have, but something that we build in a shared act of continuous creation: it's an environment in which we can be intimate. You build a friendship with the elements that you both bring to that activity — the friendship is the product of what you do with what you bring to it. What's shared is what you've built together.

Playing is one of the activities that friends can do with each other. They create an environment in which they can be playful: an environment in which they can do the kinds of things together that most of us most easily and comfortably all by ourselves — singing at the top of our lungs in the shower, making our hair into weird shapes with the shampoo, eating all of the walnuts in the gourmet chicken salad — without being paralyzed by embarrassment. It's about creating an environment where you can do all that embarrassing business without being guilt-ridden.

It's not that friends are each just doing their own, private thing in the presence of the other person; it's not voyeurism. Rather, each of them is doing something with someone else while enjoying the sense of freedom and ease that we often have only when we're alone. This is one of the forms that radical acceptance takes. Playing with your friend means that you can let your hair down, you can put your feet up, you can act and look goofy. Instead of humiliation being the turn-on, creating the environment where you can do and be who you are is the turn-on.

Of course, not all of friendship is play. But playing is a big part of it. Friends create, within the environment of the friendship that they build, a playing field. And then they're in a position to play the particular game called sex, to do sexuality together — if and when they choose. It's when sex is determined by the friendship environment that it most resembles the non-rule-governed games of early childhood: spontaneous, joyous and meaningful in the sense that it's valuable to the people who are doing it.

When sex is used to give meaning to a relationship, it often loses this wonderful playful quality — something you're doing for the fun of it — and instead is turned into a symbol of something else: whether the relationship is good or bad, whether you really love each other, how attractive you are, whether or not you're "good in bed," and all kinds of other things that carry tremendous emotional weight. You end up making it bigger than it is because of what it supposedly stands for, and less than it is because it's only something that stands for something else.

Sex is neither everything nor nothing. It's not "really" a symbol for what's real. And it's not the ultimate "reality." (Those are the two sides of the Freudian bed.) It's simply something — one of the infinite variety of activities that human beings can do together creatively or not, constructively or not, developmentally or not. The most gratifying and developmental kind of sex, in my opinion, is the physical, sensuous expression of our human capacity to share, to be giving for its own sake, minimally inhibited by societally induced shame, humiliation, or mortification. Often, it's laughing together at our own humiliation! It's part of a process that's neither depleting, nor destructive, as sex so often is in our culture of getting.

People who have attraction-based sex together are likely to relate to each other as a commodity — something to be taken care of when they first get "it" and to be taken for granted once they know "it" is theirs. Friendosexuality is, by contrast, growthful.

If you're reading this book, hopefully you will (like the people who are "in" social therapy) decide to try out the social therapeutic approach in your own way. Those of you who don't believe in premarital sex for religious or other reasons, for example, could prepare for sex after marriage by learning to be good friends with the person you plan to marry instead of using your engagement to rehearse the societal roles of husband and wife.

You may be listening for wedding bells, or preparing to celebrate your 10th, your 25th or your 50th anniversary. Maybe you're a "confirmed single," "undecided" or "none of the above." Whatever your situation, I urge that you practice friendosexuality if you want to do, build and develop rather than "have" (and be had by) good sex.

EXERCISE:

This may help you to see what it feels like when you "share your shame."

The next time you're doing sex with someone, tell each other what's most embarrassing about it. Don't wait 'til "the end" — talk while you're doing it.

10

Redoing the Past: A Few Social Therapy Success Stories and their Morals

Social therapy is at once nothing at all like traditional therapy, and very much like it. People come to us looking for emotional help, which is of course why they go to other therapists. If a therapist — any therapist — is caring and sensitive, as many are, people are touched by that and they respond; they'll decide to "go with" the therapist even if they know very little about what therapy is. What's best about therapy is that it reaches and touches people in this human and compassionate way. Where traditional therapy is less successful, in my opinion, has to do with where it goes. What's interesting and especially valuable about social therapy is where we travel with people.

Social therapy takes people on a trip. But it is not to any particular destination where everyone is supposed to end up: "higher functioning," "having greater self-awareness," "in recovery" or "living happily ever after." Rather, people who take the social therapy trip learn to go on a continuous, unlimited journey of emotional deconstruction and reconstruction: challenging the fundamental assumptions and roles of the culture of getting while reorganizing and creating their emotional lives anew.

By participating in this process you don't become a brand-new person. You acquire a new tool. Indeed, it is a new kind of tool. You become someone who is capable of building new environments where new emotions are created.

We help people to become builders, makers, creators of their lives, especially their emotional lives. This is an ongoing, lifelong process, with no end, no conclusion, and no purpose other than living life better. You could say that we teach people to build life environments that enable them to build better life environments that enable them to build ever more and ever better life environments. We have found that it is the creative activity of building — not gaining insights — that produces development and emotional growth.

Some people stay in social therapy for two sessions; some for two months; some for two years; some for two decades. People in social therapy create their own psychology and their own therapy; the varied decisions about how to do so include how much "time" it takes. Some people come for very short-term, immediate help. Others make it into a long-term part of their lives. I don't think that one way is any better than another. I want to tell you the stories of some ordinary people who continuously create social therapy even as they grow from it.

I clearly remember a very moving therapy session with Janice early on in our work. This was nearly 20 years ago. Back then Janice, who was 18 or 19 at the time, was very, very anti-authority. Not surprisingly, she was initially openly hostile toward me. So I began the session by asking her why she related to me in this way, with so much mistrust and anger. And she told me, frankly. "You're my last chance," said this angry and very unhappy young woman, who had already had two nervous breakdowns. "If this doesn't work, I'm finished — I'm gone." And I believe that she meant gone as in "I'll kill myself." Ironically, she felt that she had to stay aloof, distant from me, because the emotional stakes were too high. When she said that, it gave me a way of understanding her anger at me in a non-trivial, non-transferential way.

Let's stop a moment for a thought or two about this word "transference." In traditional Freudian and Freudian-influenced therapy, it is considered necessary for patients to go through a prolonged stage during which they "transfer" their childhood feelings toward the most significant adults in their lives onto the therapist, who can then see them, analyze them and ultimately "correct" them. Whatever reactions or responses the patient has to the therapist are interpreted in terms of transference and as evidence that the therapy is "working."

Now, in a culture of getting it is extremely common for people to relate to other human beings as other than who they are. People tend to see one another not as real and unique individuals who are valuable in and of themselves, but more as interchangeable types of things (commodities) whose value is determined by what price they can fetch on the market according to the getting principle. The social therapeutic approach does not, therefore, regard transference as a clinical technique; rather, we view it as the "normal" process that occurs for all of us living in the "normal" alienation of a culture of getting.

In saying this I am not implying that "transference" was absent from my therapeutic relationship with Janice; as I've said, given the nature of the culture of getting, transference is present in most of our societal interactions — in therapy and out of it. Again, it's the way people typically relate to one another in a commodified culture of getting. The point is that in social therapy, neither transference nor transferential analysis is "the bottom line" way of accounting for everything. We don't assume that when someone is angry at someone else it's because the anger is "really" toward a parent who was unresponsive or abusive 10, or 20, or 50 years ago. And we don't relate to our clients on the basis of this assumption — even if it's true. The social therapeutic approach practices radical acceptance; it is anti-interpretive and anti-explanatory (and very practice-able in everyday life).

Janice's anger at me came out of her fear that if I failed her she would have no place else to go. She was relating to me as who I was in her life, from her point of view. I didn't interpret, or attempt to explain, what she was saying. I accepted it — and her anger.

Janice had come to see me soon after she began going out with Howie, a client of mine who had been referred by a mutual acquaintance. Howie became my patient when he was about 18 and still living at home with his parents. Howie had had a deeply unhappy childhood. He had always been very big for his age; his family, and other people too, treated him as if he were a bull in a china shop: a fat, clumsy oaf; stupid; a bully. There's no doubt in my mind that he became a bully because he was being related to as one.

When he came into therapy he was having a lot of fights with his parents. One of the things they fought about was whether he should go on to college; he hadn't done very well in school and wasn't particularly interested in continuing. What he really wanted was to get a job in graphic design; he was already very good at that kind of work. I supported him to make the decisions he wanted to make: he moved out of his parents' apartment, and he found work in a design firm. Both were useful moves.

Howie and Janice met after he had been in therapy with me for about a year. They came to therapy together a few times. Then Janice decided to leave the therapist she had been seeing for a year or so and come into therapy with me. Eventually each of them was in individual therapy and in group therapy with me; at some point they were also in therapy as a couple.

Janice's family was more middle class than Howie's but, like him, she had had an unhappy childhood. She had been sexually abused by her father and was emotionally estranged from her family. She had the manner of someone who was "emotionally disturbed." Howie merely looked very unhappy.

When I met Howie and Janice they were emotionally unable to live very well; neither of them knew how. They found each other and social therapy almost at the same time. Now they're in their late thirties, and leading a very good life together. I think it's not unfair to say that Howie and Janice "grew up again" in social therapy. It took a long time. But that's not too surprising; after all, they had spent 17 or 18 years totally immersed in environments that were emotionally (and in Janice's case, physically) abusive, non-nourishing and deprivational.

As adults, they no longer react passively to a life determined and defined for them by their parents and other "authority" figures; they're actively engaged in the ongoing activity of creating their lives as who they are and are becoming. Howie has been very successful; he owns his own graphic design firm now and enjoys his work. Janice always had a hard time with her career, and to some extent still does. She has a teaching degree, but never especially wanted to teach; she works in a bookstore. They recently had a child — something Janice had wanted to do for a long time and that Howie wasn't sure about (they did years and years of very intense work in therapy on whether and how to become parents) — and they are both very happy about the baby, a girl. Now they're talking about having another. I think they make very good parents.

These are two people who grew up to be abnormal, miserable. That was the emotional track they were on. Janice was suicidal. I think she has a kind of willfulness, an anti-authoritarian rebelliousness, that might well have made it possible for her to kill herself. Even now, often the work with Janice comes back to her molestation when she was a child and the emotional impact that it continues to have on her. In particular, we've worked on how her unforgivingness (while understandable) tends to leave her vulnerable, in pain, and sometimes makes her mean in her behavior toward those she loves.

Howie was deeply ungratified, and emotionally undernourished. A recurring theme in his therapy is his humiliation at being related to as a big dumb kid. But he's come a long way with that. He's a loving, sensitive man — particularly by the standard of maleness in our culture. He can be, and has been, abusive to Janice. But he has a commitment to going through that, past that, and coming out the other side.

There are millions of young Americans who are like Janice and Howie were 18 years ago. At that time, no one could have expected or predicted that the two of them would succeed as they have in making a normal, satisfying life for themselves. Now they live comfortably, they have friends. They care a lot for one another, and for the baby. They're nice people. More importantly, and more accurately, they're a man and a woman who are doing some nice things with each other.

I think people get hung up sometimes on whether they and other people are "nice" or "not nice," and they allow that judgment to predetermine what they'll do with one another. I believe it works the other way around; it's what people do together, their activity, that matters. Give people a machine gun and put them in something called a "war," and they're likely to do some very awful things. Give the same people some toys and put them in a playground with a bunch of little kids and the chances are everyone will have a good time.

The social therapeutic approach has enabled Howie and Janice to learn how to build a life environment in which they can be giving to one another, which is what enables them both to grow. *Isn't their story just a case of ordinary growing up?* you may ask. *Wouldn't Janice and Howie have gotten better without social therapy?* To me the answer seems to be, plainly, no. Because they were emotionally "tracked," as so many people are. Like children who are intellectually tracked and labeled at a very early age, and whose intelligence remains undiscovered unless they are given the opportunity to express it, Janice and Howie needed to practice emotional normality in order to get "off track."

Vera is a woman in her mid-fifties who came into social therapy very briefly about a year ago, soon after her husband had had a heart attack and died. Some of Vera's friends thought that she wasn't grieving "properly." They warned her that if she didn't do it "right" now, Bill's death would "hit her" six months down the road. Her friends had succeeded in scaring her, so she came into social therapy for short-term help.

In the first of three therapy sessions, Vera told me about her life. For 28 years, she said, she and Bill had had "a good marriage, not perfect." They had built a successful art supply business together. Vera was very close to their son Paul, who had stepped in when Bill died and made sure that the business continued to run smoothly. Vera had always had an active social life, which hadn't changed. She was painting, which she loved. And she was still looking forward to taking the trip to Canada that she and Bill and several of their friends had begun planning many months before. In other words, Vera was continuing to live her life. She missed Bill a lot, but she wasn't devastated. Her friends had a hard time understanding that.

It turned out that her friends had also had a hard time understanding her marriage when Bill was alive. Vera and Bill had lived pretty independently of one another. Over the years, they had figured out a way to be together (something they both wanted) which supported each of them to be who they were rather than to act out the "normal" roles of Husband (with a capital H) and Wife (with a capital W). As Vera and I talked, it seemed to both of us that she was doing fine. She wasn't "denying" or "repressing" anything, as her amateur psychologist friends suggested; she simply

wasn't dependent on Bill in the way that her friends were dependent on their husbands. She didn't need to behave like a Widow
any more than she'd had to behave like a Wife. And there was no
reason to think that she would suddenly become paralyzed or
overwhelmed with grief if she didn't "let herself go" now. (About
four months later, just before the Canada trip, Vera came in for a
"check-up" and was still doing just fine.)

Like Vera, Gordon came into social therapy for a very brief period
of time. Like her, his reason for wanting help had to do with how
he was grieving. But their situations were very different. Six
months earlier, Gordon's life partner Norman had been killed during a robbery of the jewelry store where he had stopped to buy a
watchband. Since then, Gordon, a furniture designer, had been
unable to function. He "couldn't stop crying," he told me. When
I encouraged him to talk about what his relationship with Norman
had meant to him, and what they had done together, Gordon
could only talk about the fact that he was dead — and cry.

I suggested that their relationship might continue to grow
despite the fact of Norman's death. Not surprisingly, Gordon
thought that I was out of my mind: dead is dead. From the social
therapeutic perspective, however, the "fact of death" is yet another
fact of life. As such, it's not merely a source of grief but a building
material; it's something that can be used in the ongoing life project
of creating with whatever is at hand — even tragic death.

In the course of three more sessions, Gordon and I began to
explore what he had learned in his relationship with Norman and
how he could use that to build his relationships with other people
in a way that was developmental. That, in turn, would transform
— and develop — his relationship with his dead partner. One of
the things we talked about, for example, was letting his friends "in
on" his relationship with Norman as a way of letting them into his
life — and what it would mean for Gordon, who had always been

a "loner," to do that, given his judgments and assumptions about people, particularly men, who weren't "strong."

Gordon said he felt ashamed of being unable to handle Norman's death — of being what he called "such a wreck." In previous romantic relationships and in his friendships he had always been "the strong one," the person everyone else knew they could lean on. Norman had been the one person Gordon had allowed himself to turn to for help. Reaching out to his friends and asking for their support at this moment in his life challenged his understanding of himself, his "identity," as a man.

In accepting the challenge, Gordon decided to ask a close friend of his to come and work for him in his studio so that he wouldn't have to be alone if he suddenly felt overcome by grief, unable to lift a pen or make a phone call, as he often did. For the same reason, he accepted an invitation (which he had earlier turned down) from his sister and brother-in-law, with whom he was also close, to stay with them and their children "for as long as he wanted." Using the social therapeutic approach, he reorganized the totality of his life so that he could have the support he needed to begin growing again.

Amy, a woman in her late twenties, is a stockbroker who has been married for a year to Jon, a civil engineer. Both are very successful in their jobs. Amy came into therapy because she was having blackouts — she would find herself in strange neighborhoods very late at night, without knowing how she had gotten there and unable to remember anything about how she had spent the earlier part of the evening. Meanwhile, Jon would be at home, frantic — and then furious when she finally came in at three or four or five a.m., disheveled and obviously drunk. Amy spent the first session telling me about these "bizarre incidents," which she said had begun shortly after her marriage. They were becoming more and more frequent, and both she and her husband were very worried about them. According to Amy, the incidents were spoiling what was otherwise a "wonderful" life.

Over the next several sessions, as Amy talked about her life and her marriage, it became clear that things were something less than wonderful. In fact she had been intensely angry at Jon for many months, but felt afraid to tell him — afraid not only because she thought he would be angry at her, but because she herself believed that it was "wrong" for her to feel that way. She was deeply committed to seeing her life as being perfect and putting enormous amounts of physical and emotional energy into having it look that way to other people — which made it very difficult for her to acknowledge, to herself or anyone else, that her "ideal marriage" was not what it seemed. It took several weeks for Amy to learn and to say that she was terribly unhappy.

After about two months, Jon began coming with Amy to see me. I supported them to talk about their relationship with each other. With my encouragement, Amy was able to tell her husband the things he did that she found hurtful, and to say that she was angry with him — something she had never said to anyone in her life before this. Over the next three months, Amy and Jon worked to learn how to create a life environment in which they could talk to each other as who they were, instead of forcing their emotionality to reflect the identity of the "perfect young couple" they believed they were supposed to be. As Amy learned how she could use her anger to become closer to Jon by talking with him about how she felt, her blackouts became less and less frequent, and finally stopped.

Ironically, although Howie and Janice have been in social therapy all these years, they're both remarkably independent of it — it's been too much in their lives for them to be dependent on it. I think that if they left therapy they'd do at least as well as most people who leave when they decide that they're "cured." If and when they want to leave, of course, I'll support them to do it. But they're not in any hurry; they've built the therapy into their life activity. It's just one of the things they do, like other people go to a health club. Howie and Janice come to their respective therapy groups once a week to "work out" emotionally. And they're in pretty good shape, as you are when you exercise regularly.

I've been with them, and they've been with me, half their lives. In some ways, they and social therapy have grown up together. Howie and Janice came when social therapy itself was fairly "young," theoretically and organizationally. And they've participated in nourishing it, in giving to it. They've contributed significantly to the social therapy process; through all its ebbs and flows, zigs and zags, they've gone along with and created it. I think if there's any "secret" to their success, it's that from the beginning they've been enormously generous in their posture and their attitude despite the fact that, emotionally speaking, they didn't have a whole lot at first.

They're both completely giving as patients. Janice, for example, does not come "naturally" to group. But she's always worked to be there, to be giving of her emotionality. They both gave what they had, which at first was their pain, their anger, their not knowing, their humiliation. And we worked, together with other people, to build something with all of that emptiness and ugliness — to make something that could be helpful not only to them, but to a whole lot of folks.

They've been vital to the development of what we do — they're major builders of social therapy. And in that process of giving, of building, both of them have grown. They're "model" patients not in the sense that they're "stars" or emotionally extraordinary, but in the sense that they've been tremendously helped "merely" by giving to this process — not only in order to get help, but to give help. Now there are many people like that. Howie and Janice were simply two of the first.

Yet Howie and Janice didn't just "happen" to get cured because they'd been around for a long time, or because "they got in on the ground floor." And while it's great that these two extremely decent people, who were well on their way to emotional death (and, in Janice's case, maybe physical death as well), are now very much alive, the point is not that their story is having a happy ending because they had social therapy "done to" them, or even because they made a contribution to "it."

Howie and Janice did much more than make a contribution; they helped to make the "anti-institution" of social therapy what it is. Their cure is inseparable from their participation in the activity of creating a new psychology — which is, in fact, what it means to be "in" social therapy. As Howie and Janice continue to develop, they have more and more to give to the development of social therapy, which is thereby increasingly able to help them to develop further. This is how the social therapeutic approach works, and anyone — a household, a group of friends, lovers — can practice it. You can use this approach to create a new, human psychology. And in doing that activity you will, like Howie and Janice, Vera, Gordon, Amy and Jon, reinitiate your development.

You may be wondering why I'm going out of my way to insist that what's needed is to create our own psychology. That's because the Clinical Psychology (capital C and capital P) we currently have — Freudian and Freudian-influenced psychology — has proven itself to be remarkably unhelpful to human beings from a developmental, and therefore from a human, perspective.

The self-appointed task of traditional clinical psychology is to measure the extent to which people are "maladjusted" and to talk them (increasingly to drug them) into adjusting to the existing roles and rules of society. At its often coercive "best," psychology enables people like Howie and Janice, Vera, Gordon, Amy and Jon to fit in; it doesn't "know how" to help anyone to develop because, in my opinion, it doesn't really "believe in" human development.

And that's the trouble with psychology. It relates to people as if we were like the stars, rocks, insects and atoms which are the objects that the physical sciences study. Now it makes perfect sense to me that the science of physics, for example, with its generalizable laws and body of knowledge and interconnected formal paradigms (problem-solution, causal explanation, prediction) should be applied to physical objects. Such objects may go through profound changes, but they're incapable — as far as anyone can tell — of developing in the way that Howie and Janice continue to do. The instruments for studying the non-human world may change, but the method of study — like the object — fundamentally does not. In fact, I believe that the physical sciences have been so extraordinarily successful in part because the "fit" between their method and their subject is so close.

And that is precisely why, in my opinion, a clinical psychology that imitates the physical sciences is doomed to failure: Howie and Janice are growing (up) again, but traditional psychology can't "imagine" it — let alone create the conditions for it to happen. I think we need a human science, a psychology, which is different from the natural sciences for the simple and seemingly obvious reason that human beings are fundamentally different from the rest of nature, from the physical world, even as we are part of it. A psychology that mirrors the natural sciences, therefore, denies what is most characteristic of the human object of psychology (Howie, Janice, Vera, Gordon, Amy, Jon and the rest of us) — our unique capacity to develop and to grow. Imagine a science of ornithology which didn't take into account the fact that birds fly!

In other words, we need to create a science of psychology that's at least as appropriate to the object it studies (all of us and our lives) as astronomy is to the stars, or as geology is to the earth. What that means, in my opinion, is a psychology which is itself capable of continuous development. If it isn't, then it's not relevant to our lives. It's no better than a myth — regardless of the credentials, and even the good intentions, of its practitioners.

Social therapy's fundamental commitment is not to the preservation of social therapy. That's what I mean when I say that social therapy is an anti–institution. It's not a fixed thing that clients or patients are invited to contribute to or that they are included in; it's a life activity — the continuous creation of a new psychology — by everyone who chooses to participate, in whatever way they choose to do it.

By creating a new psychology, I don't mean "a search for a new way of talking" about psychology. This is how some very talented and committed colleagues recently described their therapeutic work: they call patients "guests," they allow them to "own" the therapy, they focus on "solution talk" rather than "problem talk." The social therapeutic approach is doing something much more radical! We're teaching people like Howie and Janice, Vera, Gordon, Amy and Jon to create environments where they can create not just solutions to problems, or even new emotions, but a new emotionality and a new psychology. We have discovered that this activity is both possible and curative. Not only are Howie and Janice developing, they're developing the activity called social therapy, which is helping them to develop and grow even further.

EXERCISE:

Here's how you can practice creating an environment where people are supported to create something new.

Get together with a good friend or friends and go someplace you've never gone together. Tell each other how it feels to be there.

11

'Addiction' Versus Development

My perspective on "addiction" (at this point, I'm sure you won't be surprised to hear) is that there is no such thing. What there is, of course, is a multi-billion dollar addictions industry, which is enormously lucrative despite the fact that it deals in myth. Moreover, the various treatment plans (12-step and others) which claim to "treat" the "addicted" are remarkably unsuccessful — even on their own terms. For example, success rates for so-called drug and alcohol "addiction" programs are often put at less than 10% by these programs themselves!

Yet despite its failure, the "addiction" model is virtually everywhere. Having begun by being used in the treatment of "alcoholism," and then drug use, it's now frivolously and hurtfully used to label everyone from people who gamble to "women who love too much." Which only goes to show that what tends to count in the "addictions" business is frequently determined more by how much money is made on a particular kind of treatment than by how many people — if any — are ever helped by it.

It's ironic (not to mention hypocritical) that while the official outcry against so-called street drugs has gotten louder and louder, the psychiatric profession is more and more throwing itself into the business of peddling drugs full-time. Drugs — the legal as well as the illegal kind — are very big business in America. The American Psychiatric Association and the major pharmaceutical companies apparently have nothing against people with a drug "dependency" — as long as the "addicts" (or their insurance companies) are paying for it.

"Our tests show that your little boy is 'hyperactive' and he suffers from 'attention deficit disorder.' Give him Ritalin every morning with his orange juice and every night with his milk and cookies," some specialist may say. "He'll soon calm down and start paying attention."

"You're depressed," another might advise. "Pop a Prozac every day for the rest of your life and you'll feel a lot more cheerful."

From a social therapeutic vantage point, the "addiction" label is typically an alternative to — indeed, in opposition to — human development. "Addiction" talk is not benign. It's often positively painful.

Now, to say there's no such thing as "addiction" — to say that "addiction" is a myth — is not in any way to deny that there are millions of Americans who engage in drinking and drug-taking behavior that's often (although not always) destructive to themselves and other people. But no one, in my opinion, has ever produced any evidence or argument to show that the term "addiction" or the label "addict" has any explanatory or curative value. Nor has anyone shown that conventional methods of dealing with "addiction" are effective except in a tragically small handful of cases. Those methods are based on a pseudo-medical model that views such behavior as symptomatic of a biochemically or genetically influenced disease of which "addicts" can never effectively be cured. This, presumably, is why the term "recovered" is used —

to show that they can always have a "relapse."

The extraordinary failure of the addictions industry to help people "kick" the drinking or drug "habit" has not, of course, deflated the myth of addiction. On the contrary, many Americans now believe that people can be "addicted" to just about anything: sugar, horse racing, sex — even other people, including people who are "addicted" to something else!

But, again, no evidence exists, in my opinion, for thinking that there is such a thing as "addiction" or that it explains anything. Nor is there any evidence for thinking that it helps people to "know" they belong to a category of human beings that the "specialists" call "addicts." Such classification serves no developmental purpose (once an "addict," always an "addict") but is useful for social control. The medicalization of "addiction" — packaging it as a particular "problem" located in particular individuals — disguises the societal causes of destructive drinking and drug-taking by blaming the "addicts." And while placing the blame on the "addict" it also, ironically, takes the responsibility off her or his shoulders.

What the evidence does show is that people drink alcohol, or ingest or inject chemicals into their bodies, to make themselves "tranquil," to get "high," to "feel good" or to "forget" because they think they have nothing better to do. By "better" I don't mean morally superior, but more effective — they don't know of any more effective way to deal with the chronic and often extreme emotional pain that so many of us live with, day in and day out: shame and humiliation, rage, panic and anxiety, depression and alienation. In 20-plus years of doing social therapy with people who were treated (usually unsuccessfully) elsewhere for drug and alcohol abuse — including business executives, inner-city teenagers, suburban housewives, professional dancers, elementary school teachers, social workers and men with long-term prison records — I've never yet met anyone who drank or took drugs for any other reason than that he or she chose to do so.

Not surprisingly, however, people who are classified as "addicts" get just as caught up in the myth of addiction as everyone else tends to do. Instead of taking responsibility for making the particular choices they have made, they often choose to become "addicted" to "addiction."

Ginny is one of them. Back in April of 1990, she came to a talk I gave in New York City whose title was "The Politics and Psychology of Addiction." A woman in her forties who had recently stopped doing drugs again after using them most of her life (she had "stopped" many times before), Ginny was at first outraged by my characterization of "addiction" as a myth. Her whole life was organized around the fact that she had either conquered (or failed to conquer) her "addiction." A skilled social worker, the mother of a teenage daughter, and a talented writer, Ginny nevertheless saw herself ("identified" herself) primarily as a victim who had managed (sometimes) to overcome her drug "problem" but was still only one "hit" away from being the person she had been for 30 years.

Ginny eventually decided — made a choice — to come into a social therapy group, where we intensified our efforts to deal with her "addiction" to "addiction." At first Ginny insisted that there are certain kinds of people who have a drinking or a drug "problem" — a "dependency" — that defines who they are. It's the very essence of their identity even after they stop the behavior associated with it — "former drug addicts" and "recovered alcoholics" — and it overdetermines their life activity. If they give in even once to the temptation of a drink, or a sniff, according to Ginny, the quicksand of their "addiction" will pull them under again.

Ginny's way of understanding herself, and this way of understanding human beings in general, is, in my opinion, enormously damaging. The so-called 12-step programs might more accurately be described as a "Catch-22." These programs are explicitly designed to prevent the "alcoholic" or the "addict" from ever taking another drink again — instead of helping people to deal effectively with what happens when they do take another drink, which is (even according to the 12-step entrepreneurs themselves) far more likely to occur. By the self-serving, pseudo-medical definitions of such programs, one drink and you're right back where you started: an "alcoholic" who needs — you guessed it — to begin at the first step all over again. That's what I mean when I say that the myth of addiction is an alternative to development. By their own logic, these programs often lead their graduates to think that if they "make the mistake" of taking even one drink they may as well drink as much as they like. After all, the reasoning goes, one drink is enough to "trigger" the "addiction" — so why not go all the way?

By contrast, the social therapeutic approach does not involve any attempts to work on anyone's drinking "problem" or drug "problem." Nor do we put people who drink too much, or people who "do" drugs, in separate groups where they can talk about their "addiction" openly because only other "addicts" could possibly understand them. "Addicts," by this logic, are "addicted" to talking only to other "addicts." We don't make the assumption that someone who drinks heavily or takes drugs has nothing to contribute to a group that includes people who don't do those things, or vice versa. We don't reduce people to their "problems" or their "addictions."

The reality is that a person who shoots heroin or drinks a fifth of bourbon or consumes substantial amounts of Valium every day also does, and cares about, all kinds of other things. She or he makes choices; the life of someone who shoots heroin or drinks bourbon or takes Valium is — like everyone else's — a complex and ever-changing totality. It's simply not scientifically valid to define that totality in terms of a particular behavior or characteristic.

This is also true of people with severe mental or physical illness, who are often and oppressively related to in our culture as if they were only their "madness" or their "disability" — as if they didn't have choices and responsibilities. I am among those who believe that Freudian psychology, by creating an approach which included entering into a social contract with the so-called "madman" and "madwoman," made an enormous advance from the inhuman pre-20th century practices associated with the belief that "crazy" people were possessed by the devil. But I don't think we can settle today for what was "progressive" in 1904.

The fact is that every one of us — heavy drinkers, drug takers, and "crazy" people no less than anyone else — still has to figure out how we're going to live our lives, hour by hour, day by day, and year by year. Like the rest of us, they too must ask the development question. If life is to be developmental, human beings must be continuously engaged in transforming totalities, recreating ourselves — not changing particular behaviors. Changing behavior is what the conventional treatment of "addiction" attempts to do, and that, in my opinion, is why it almost always fails.

The social therapeutic approach has been enormously successful in helping people to see that they can make other life choices. Surprisingly, it is easier and more developmentally effective to change who you are totally than to change any particular behavior.

One of those people is Robert, who had a nervous breakdown during his second year in law school and spent the next several years drinking himself into a stupor so that he wouldn't have to experience his humiliation. Now in his late thirties, Robert is a very successful high school English teacher. He has learned that he doesn't have to live his life on the basis of his identity as a failed lawyer or a successful alcoholic.

Jessie is another social therapeutic success story: she is a 55-year-old nurse who at one time in her life drank so heavily that she couldn't keep a job and was living on the streets. After graduating from a 12-step program, Jessie lived practically like a recluse for fear that if she went out socially she would be "tempted" to start drinking again. In social therapy, Jessie eventually came to see that she could decide whether to drink alcohol and, if she decided to drink, to decide when, where and how. She is currently leading a very active life, occasionally taking a glass of wine at dinner or a drink at a party. She's been doing so for years. She's learned how to live a life that includes drinking without being overdetermined by it and overidentified with it. From the social therapeutic perspective, the issue is not whether Jessie drinks or doesn't drink, but how she's living the totality of her life.

The same is true of Pam, a working class woman in her thirties, who began doing heroin when she was a teenager. When she was in her twenties, Pam agreed to enter a methadone program that was ostensibly an alternative to prison (she had been arrested for robbery) but turned out to be nearly as coercive. Pam had been on methadone for several years when she came into social therapy (over the objections of her drug counselor). She rapidly decided to stop taking drugs, completed a bachelor's degree in art and a master's degree in social work, and is fulfilling her lifelong dream of doing art therapy with kids.

Then there is Tom, who "went crazy" as a young man, was hospitalized and sent through the traditional treatment "mill." For 14 years Tom was on Thorazine. Overweight, slow-moving, and with a condition known as tardive dyskinesia — an involuntary muscular movement that caused him to lick his lips constantly (an extremely common, often permanent, side effect of drugs like Thorazine) — Tom seemed doomed to a victim's life of isolation and misery. Yet after being in social therapy for a few years, he decided to go off Thorazine. His whole life "picked up" — he got a decent job, lost weight, and when last heard from (he left social therapy about a year later) was happily married.

There is no moral to these stories, or happy endings. For

Ginny, Robert, Jessie, Pam and Tom, as for the rest of us, life goes on. It isn't divided into beginnings, middles and ends (or chapters, or "steps"); life is to be lived, as responsibly and developmentally as we can do it, not explained or labeled.

People frequently ask me if I am absolutely opposed to someone using various legal (prescription and non-prescription) drugs. They are often surprised to hear that I am not. If drugs are useful to people in pain, and if they seem to have no adverse side effects or are helpful in treatment, I see no earthly reason to reject them. They're just part of what modern medical science and technology have created, and some of them are no less than miraculous.

No. I am not anti-drug; I do not believe that most drugs are necessarily inconsistent with development. But if development isn't part of the prescription, then I urge that you *just say no.*

I am not anti-classification; many advances in modern medicine are inextricably linked to carefully researched, functional classification. But I *am* unequivocally opposed to pseudo-classification (what I call labeling). It creates an imaginary disease ("addiction") that is both subtly and not so subtly a moral category pretending to be a medical one, blaming people more than describing them in a useful way. And, at the same time, labeling implies that people are not responsible for their life decisions. In blaming people while absolving them of responsibility, labeling is wholly and perniciously anti-developmental.

Calling someone an "addict" is anti-developmental because, in my opinion, it effectively denies people both the responsibility and the possibility of continuing to create and transform themselves and their environments. Labels like "addict" and "addiction" are anti-human moral imperatives dressed up in pseudo-medical, pseudo-scientific clothing. I have no "problem" with people choosing religion. But it must be properly "labeled."

EXERCISE:

This is a way to take a break from a habit you don't like so that you can look at it from a distance.

For one day, whenever you feel like doing something that's a habit (chewing gum, biting your nails, smoking or whatever) reread this chapter instead.

12

Whose Pain Is It, Anyway?

In our culture of getting, it's "only natural," or at least not surprising, that most of us learn to hold on to everything we can — even if we don't regard what we've got as a particularly good thing. Our possessive relationship to pain, the "my-ness" of physical and emotional pain, is a particularly good example of this: we typically don't think it's desirable that we're in pain, but we do insist that it's "ours." We possess it even though it hurts like hell!

The "my-ness" of pain is one of many philosophical, linguistic and cultural assumptions that gets deconstructed in the social therapeutic process. For it doesn't necessarily follow from the fact that you're feeling it that the pain is "yours," any more than it follows from the fact that you're living in a beautiful house that it's yours. If you think it is, check with the bank!

In many life situations, individuals produce outcomes that are attributed to the group; when a baseball player hits a home run, for instance, it's officially chalked up to the team. Sports reporters' fixation on the statistics and history of individual baseball players is, of course, not actually a part of the game. It's an accompaniment to the game.

In social therapy we challenge the deeply held cultural assumption that pain — by its very nature — is something which only individuals can possess. I believe that relating to pain (emotional and physical) in this culturally prescribed way actually intensifies it. Characteristically, the person who feels pain is also supposed to be the one who takes responsibility for dealing with it. If you have a headache (or a heartache), you're the one who's expected to "report" it (or not); you're supposed to decide who else (if anyone) needs to know about it; it's your job to find and consult "experts" on this kind of pain, to weigh their advice, and to apply what you think are the appropriate remedies until you get better. Being "alone" with pain magnifies people's subjective experience of it.

In a social therapeutic environment, people are helped to socialize pain. That is, social therapy teaches people to give up the "private ownership" of pain by giving "their" pain to the group, if the group will accept it. That activity transforms what pain is.

How can that be? Well, pain is no different from other things in that what you do with it determines to a large extent what it is. After all, you can hit someone over the head with a baseball bat, or use a silk tie as a tourniquet to save a person's life. I'm not suggesting that the socialization of physical and emotional pain does away with it; the sharing of pain is not an anesthetic, or a placebo intended to make people think that they're in less pain than they "really" are. What we have found is that socializing pain changes people's experience of it.

Joyce, a patient in social therapy, is a middle class woman in her early thirties who has suffered from migraine headaches since she was a teenager. Along with the physical symptoms that are typical of such headaches — throbbing pain, nausea, extreme tiredness — she became anxious and upset, Joyce told her therapy group, whenever she felt one coming on, in part because she didn't know what to do or how to act. If she was at work, should she take some pills and pretend that she "just" had a headache, or try to lie down, or go home? If she was at home, should she call in sick? When she was alone, she told us, she would sometimes "moan and groan," and then blame herself for "acting like a baby." Sometimes she worried that she might have a brain tumor which had gone undiagnosed. She wondered if she should be more active in exploring new treatments for migraine, or if she had to "learn to live with it" (as one physician had advised her to do).

After weeks of therapeutic work, the social therapy group — including Joyce — decided that she should no longer be the "owner" of her pain. She would let us know, to the extent possible (we were not always accessible), whenever she had a headache or felt one coming. And we would take collective responsibility for it. We would take it over. Should she take the pills? Close her eyes? Lie down? Someone else — maybe everyone else — could moan for her.

This is a good (although simple) example of what social therapy means by completing: you indicate your pain, and the whole group moans. In this way, we challenge the assumption that pain is something people have to have (or do, or know how to deal with) alone by transforming the traditional organization of pain — emotional and physical — as a privately owned experience. We reorganize it as a social activity. How can that make a difference? In the same way that the reorganization of sex as individual, private behavior changes what it is; the social activity of making love with another person may not necessarily be "more" or "less," "better" or "worse," than masturbating, but the subjective experience of it is very different — even when the objective biochemical character of both may be identical.

This is all very well and good, you may be thinking. *But it doesn't really change the pain...When push comes to shove, Joyce is still the one whose head is killing her.* Well, yes and no. Look at it this way: for many hundreds of thousands of years, the remains of long-dead plants and animals that we use in the form of coal, oil and natural gas lay buried deep in the earth. It wasn't until the invention of tools and techniques specifically designed to extract it that fossil fuel could "become" what it is now. The stuff itself is what it had been for ages; it's also transformed. The interaction between that dead matter and the technology reorganized what there was and made it something new. Socialized, Joyce's pain is as much the same as it had been, and as different, as that.

It's this subjective dimension of pain which has been more or less ignored by traditional medicine. Now there's no doubt that modern medical science has made many impressive advances in treating disease as a result of its attention to the "objective" causes of pain. We can all be deeply thankful for medicine; it has saved countless lives. Yet I believe we could go much further in helping people who suffer from physical illness if we were more attentive to the subjective experience and reorganization of pain. Many physicians acknowledge that pain is the product of a complex set of conditions rather than a single factor. More importantly, once someone is in pain, that new condition (being in pain) becomes part of the "set"; it is a factor — often an important one — in determining what happens next. The social reorganization of pain, therefore, can have a significant impact on the conditions that originally caused it.

Recently I began doing a weekly social therapy group with a number of seriously ill people who are outpatients at a large private hospital in New York City. There are about 10 people in the group; most are poor women in their fifties and sixties, although one or two are considerably younger. Several have diabetes, one woman in her twenties has AIDS, and others have cancer, cerebral palsy and heart disease. Although nearly every one of them started out talking very "politely" about how well she was being taken care of by her doctors, how supportive her family was, and what strength she derived from her religious beliefs, it became clear almost from the beginning that nearly all of them are quite angry.

They're angry at the "powers-that-be" (indifferent hospital administrators and insensitive doctors). They're angry at husbands and children and grandchildren who still expect to be taken care of: "They say how concerned they are, but I'm still the one who's getting the supper every night — seems like I'm the only one in that house who can't be tired." They're angry at people who are healthy: "Why me and not her?" They're angry at other sick people in their lives and in the group: "My disease is a tragedy, but your disease is your fault." And it seems to me that, even though they rarely admit it, they're deeply angry at themselves — and humiliated — because they were "irresponsible" in how they lived their lives and thereby made themselves sick. Most of the women find these feelings, particularly their anger at themselves, enormously painful, stressful, and very difficult to express.

How do sick people get sick? There's plenty of evidence to indicate that environmental factors, broadly speaking — pollution of the air and water, food additives, inadequate health care and poor nutrition, societal tensions, antagonisms and fears — all play a major role in determining that large numbers of people will get sick, and the kinds of diseases they're likely to have. There's also ample evidence to show that, given those conditions, the life decisions and choices made by individuals largely determine who will get sick and how sick they will be.

So I think sick people are justifiably furious in many, perhaps most, cases. The trouble is that they're the ones who are most likely to be further destroyed by their rage at others, and by the self-hatred and the humiliation that they feel. My concern, as a social therapist, is to help these people who are sick to give healthy expression to their feelings — to use their feelings developmentally.

Among other things, severe illness can be an occasion for further coming to terms with the question of who you are by engaging the sometimes very painful question of how you got sick and continue to be sick — to look at what you did to wind up and remain in this possibly life-threatening (or, at least, quality of life-diminishing) situation. This is never for the purpose of getting people to see that they are to blame, or to deny that other societal and biological factors are involved. It's to enable them to come to understand and transform who they are.

In a social therapy group, the question is always whether we can create a relatively guilt-free environment — that is, an environment in which judgments do not overdetermine the activity. For it is only under such conditions that each person can give what she "owns" — including her physical and emotional pain, her fear, her "stupidity" (what she did that she thinks contributed to her becoming ill) and her anger — to the group. That's the social therapeutic activity.

Sylvia, a woman in her late forties who recently came into a social therapy group, had just been diagnosed with diabetes. One night in group I asked her how things were going in connection with her health.

She told us that her doctor had been recommending various ways in which she could do something about the diabetes in addition to the medical treatment — eating differently, exercising — but that "nothing worked."

Tom, another patient in the group, was immediately sympathetic. He said we should work to figure out something — "even something very small" — that Sylvia could definitely do so she would have some immediate success in dealing with her diabetes. It would be good for her, Tom thought, to have that experience.

I asked Tom whether he believed that Sylvia was doing everything she could to deal with her health situation. He said he didn't — he thought she was being "negative." So I asked him why he hadn't said that to Sylvia. After all, if she's being "negative" in her response to having diabetes, it was likely that she would negativize whatever we gave her — however "small."

Sylvia was saying, in effect: "I'd like to be cured of diabetes without changing at all." From the standpoint of traditional medicine, that sort of makes sense. Traditional medicine, like Sylvia herself, sees: 1. Sylvia (that's Sylvia as she Ought To Be). 2. Sylvia-with-diabetes (that's the Problem). 3. Sylvia-cured-of-diabetes/ Sylvia-back-to-normal (that's the Solution).

The social therapeutic approach sees Sylvia very differently. From this point of view, if she wants to maximize her chances of being cured there has to be a developmental transformation on Sylvia's part. She has to reorganize the totality of her life, which now includes diabetes but is not limited to the fact that she has a serious illness. Such a transformation can have a real impact on the diabetes itself, *and* on the quality of Sylvia's life as well.

You see, if she's going to do something about diabetes (and this goes for diseases such as cancer and AIDS also), Sylvia can't abstract it from the totality of her life. She has to develop and grow as who she is, including the diabetes.

Diabetes. AIDS. Cancer. A stroke. You've just heard the news about yourself or someone you love, and it's bad. Are you looking at months, or years, of disability, pain and suffering? Will it end in death? No matter what, this is very serious business.

What makes it particularly hard for people when they get old, or find out that they have a debilitating, possibly fatal illness (old age and disease often go together), is that these situations or conditions tend to be related to as being something other than a period of their lives. But that is what they are: old age and serious illness are as much "moments" in our lives — particular moments, but moments nevertheless — as any other. For a baseball player, the first week of the season is different from the last week. Yet it's also true that the hits he gets at the end are given the same weight as the hits he gets in the beginning when they figure out his annual statistics and his lifetime batting average.

From the social therapeutic perspective, the quality of life (how you play the living game, not what the clock or the calendar says) is the issue. How do we handle the end of a love affair, the birth of a child, a quarrel with a friend, the news that we have a malignant tumor? This is not in any way to trivialize or deny the physical and emotional pain of being seriously ill, but to point out that as human beings (and this is what makes us different from all other forms of life) we are always in the position of being able to choose how we live (in sickness and in health) until the moment when we're no longer alive. All of us have to decide how we're going to shape and organize and give expression to the complex experience that is life. And that issue is as relevant for people who are living the last two years of life as it is to those who are living the first 25 years.

We probably all know people who are in excellent health but who aren't getting a whole lot out of life at all. Being healthy doesn't come with a guarantee against misery, and being very sick doesn't require or "mean" that who you are is reducible to the sickness. It is a fact of life that dying (of old age, or of illness) is like any other situation in that it can be the occasion for profound development. In Marie's case it was.

Marie came into social therapy with me when she was in her late forties and working as an editor for a publishing company. Marie had been unhappily married, twice, and was the mother of a teenage son with whom she wasn't very close. She complained that her mother and older sisters and brothers still treated her as "the baby of the family." In fact, Marie was babyish; like many people do, she had spent much of her life "waiting around" to get something from someone — her family, the men in her life, her son — but hardly anyone had ever come through for her. She hadn't gotten very much from any of them, and she was bitter, resentful and self-pitying because of that. She tried, not very successfully, to hide all this beneath a joking, "life of the party" manner.

About a month after she started therapy, Marie was diagnosed with ovarian cancer. She had a hysterectomy, and for a year or two the cancer went into remission. Then it recurred and eventually metastasized throughout her body. During these years we worked together with the other members of her social therapy group to help Marie figure out how she wanted to live her life, given that she was very seriously ill.

It became increasingly clear to all of us, including Marie, that her life strategy of getting hadn't gotten her very far and that she had nothing to lose from trying a different game plan. When she died, at the age of 56, Marie had learned how to give; in the last two or three years of her life she simply gave and gave and gave. This became the most developmental and gratifying moment of her life; I was very close to her during this time and, believe me, she had a ball.

Marie became enormously giving, but it wasn't easy. Her family didn't approve; they put enormous pressure on her to stay a victim so that they could be victims also. "Why did this have to happen to you?" her mother cried. "Why did you have to do this to me?"

"You have cancer," they would remind her in one way or another (as if it might have slipped her mind). "You're dying. You don't owe anyone anything. Everyone should be doing for you. Now, of all times, you should be getting, not giving."

But that doesn't even make sense according to the logic of getting, because when you're dying of cancer nothing you could get would make a difference to you (compensate you for your suffering). In social therapy, we believe that "now of all times" (when you're in a great deal of pain and you know that you're going to die sooner rather than later) is exactly when you should be most giving.

Why? Because (like everyone else) you've got to do *something* between now and then, and living to get just isn't that good for your mental (or physical) health. The social therapeutic approach is to say to someone who is very old, or terminally ill: Given these circumstances, what do you want to do (to give) for the next three months or six months or two years?

When the cancer first came back, Marie thought about killing herself. We talked about it in her social therapy group. Marie said that she didn't have moral or religious scruples against committing suicide, but it was clearly not a very giving activity. By this time, she had already begun trying to live according to the giving principle.

There were some people (most of her relatives) who said Marie was crazy, and others (most of her friends) who said she was "a saint" to live her life this way. But Marie was neither out of her mind, nor out of this world. She was just a decent, ordinary woman who, with support, decided that she wanted to continue to develop and to grow. Her death was an issue for some of the people in her life who were given to, but not in the same way as it was for her.

At the beginning, Marie wanted to know what she would get out of being giving. But that's never the social therapeutic question — not because we think it's "selfish," but because we don't think anyone is particularly helped by asking it. In social therapy, the question is always: What are you going to give to it? And that's regardless of what the "it" is. The social therapeutic approach doesn't rest on an investment model; we don't advocate giving because it has a "high yield" or produces a particular result: "Do it because you'll get something out of it." Rather, we advocate living and dying to be giving because that's how human beings develop.

So Marie discovered how to be giving of everything that she was — including her cancer — all the time. No matter how sick someone may be, the sickness or the pain is never all there is in his or her life. Being in pain, even when it's excruciating, just isn't all we are. People needn't stop living when they find out that they're dying; it needn't totally consume them. Even people on their deathbeds, who are hours away from being dead, are engaged in all kinds of life activities: they argue, they reminisce, they complain, they apologize, they forgive; they're intensely involved in living. People can be in enormous pain and still watch a baseball game on television, read a book, take part in a conversation, laugh at a joke.

One of the nice things about giving is that it's never too late to give and you can never give too much. A fundamental principle of the social therapeutic approach is that your life — whatever "time" it is, regardless of the circumstances — will be gratifying to the extent that you give.

The socialization of pain has an impact on everyone who participates; it supports the people who are not in physical pain to expose and to give "their" emotionality to others, and to engage their limitations in doing so. Some members of Joyce's social therapy group — including Joyce — were initially skeptical. "It's still her (my) pain," they said in knee-jerk fashion — meaning that what pain really is, after all, is the privatized experience of it. But although pain *includes* the personal experience of it, it's not reducible to that.

The subjective experience or perception of pain (or sex or anything else, for that matter) — isn't "natural," or "raw" — it's always shaped by our culture (our way of seeing and feeling). The evidence of many anthropological studies clearly indicates that pain is experienced and performed quite variously in different cultures. We do pain in a privatized, competitive way in our culture of getting; social therapy is a cultural and therapeutic experience which supports people to do pain socially and completitively instead.

Although Joyce's pain has become substantially less, it isn't all gone. She still possesses it — the group's work still isn't finished. It never is. Life goes on.

EXERCISE:

This gives you a way to see how it feels when you give away your pain.

Trade illnesses with a friend or a member of your family — figure out when, where and how to get help for them, and let them do the same for you.

13

Small Change

Acquiring and spending money are, perhaps, the showcase activities of a culture of getting. It simply isn't possible to confine these "money acts" and the "meanings" connected to them to the sphere of economics; they're intertwined with all aspects of personal and emotional life. You may be able to keep money out of your bedroom (which isn't so easy), but you surely can't keep it out of your whole house.

If money were only a medium of exchange (as the economists say) — something that gives people access to what can be bought with it — then it would make perfect sense for everybody to try to get as much of it as necessary in order to have the things that we need and want. Some people might end up with more money, and they'd be able to buy more than the people who had less of it. This might lead to certain disagreements, but it wouldn't necessarily *mean* anything about the people who had more — or the people who had less.

But money in our society is much else besides being a medium of exchange. The trouble with money isn't that it's used to buy things (most of us would find it inconvenient to barter goods and services in exchange for our daily bread), but that it's used as a social measure for assessing how good a getter someone is. In fact, how much money we have is, arguably, the ultimate test in our culture of our value as human beings. And that's what makes money (and the absence of it) if not the root of all evil, a source of tremendous guilt, anger and humiliation.

In our culture of getting, what we get out of spending money is not just the things that we purchase but our own and other people's judgments (approval, disapproval, admiration, contempt and a host of others) about how good we are at making money and at using it. People who live in the "best" ("exclusive") neighborhoods, wear expensive clothes and jewelry, and go to places where it costs a lot to get in are likely to be rated (if not openly, at least implicitly) as superior human beings who deserve to have everything that they have. Among other things, it's assumed that they have the "good taste" to "appreciate" it. Indeed, they define what "taste" is.

The other side of the coin, of course, is that people who don't have enough money to buy the best of everything are also judged accordingly. They're often regarded as inferior human beings (ordinary people) whose lack of money is not just a fact but a sign of something — which is that they don't deserve to have it. We find it difficult to accept that the street person may be substantially smarter than the president of a Major Corporation — or that we, sitting at home and watching the news on TV, may have a better feel for what's going on in the world than the Major Network anchorman or anchorwoman who's telling us about it.

Money is used not just to measure the value of people who are very rich and very poor; *all* of us are judged according to how much or how little we have and how we spend it. That's a dehumanizing and degrading test, regardless of the grade we get. As such it is an extremely painful issue for many, many people. It isn't easy to be jolly during the Christmas season, for example, if you feel that you aren't a real man because you're unable to measure up to what the magazine and television ads say you should be able to buy for your wife and children.

Now from my perspective, there's nothing unhealthy, in a getting culture, about people working to get as much money as possible so they can buy as much as possible. But it's not conducive to our mental health and development when we're knocking ourselves out (or knocking other people on the head) to get and spend money as a way of proving our worth as human beings: to show the world, and ourselves, how intelligent, good, morally upright and valuable we are. It's one thing to get the money to get the new house. It's quite another thing to think that such getting gets you everything.

Moreover, the fact that having money is often taken to be the most important sign of people's worth in a culture of getting has major consequences for how easy it is for them to get more. The truism that "money makes (begets) money" happens to be true. The more you have of it, the greater the likelihood that you'll be given access to more. The less you have, the less likely it is that you'll gain access to any. Are you a B+ getter or a C- getter? It's not only a matter of appearances (how good you look as a getter); how good you *are* as a getter (which is often symbolized by how good you look) can make all the difference in the world.

Family members therefore engage in endless debates over what is the right way to invest what they have so that they can get more. Summer camp for the kids? A new car? Fixing up the house? And they continuously criticize one another's attitude toward money; whether or not you have the "right" attitude could determine how much more money you can get.

Over the years, I've worked therapeutically with many couples and families who spent much of their time fighting over the "right" way to spend money. When people view how they and others spend money as a measure of the kind of human beings they are, then the language they use to talk about it is often the abusive language of moral judgments: they accuse each other of being "irresponsible," of not knowing "the value of money," of not caring what the neighbors think or of caring too much. What gets called into question isn't just how much money the other person is spending, or on what, but who this person is: "What kind of father would deny his child..." "Why would a woman buy two..." "How could he..." "What could she be thinking of..."

Here's a small change I suggest people make in how they relate to each other about money; it can make a big difference. Remember this basic economic fact of life: Money doesn't equal value! Accept the fact that people differ from one another, often a great deal, in their values, tastes and desires and in how they give expression to them. Some people consider occasional luxuries (a cab ride home, cashmere gloves, steak instead of hamburger for dinner, a long-distance call to a friend in the middle of the day) to be valuable necessities. Others place a high value on having savings in the bank. Values vary dramatically. Money is a relative constant. If you measure people's wildly divergent values by money, you're being ungiving in a way that, in my opinion, makes intimacy all but impossible.

I think it's very important for people who have money in common to learn how to talk with each other openly and honestly about their value differences without being overdetermined by their judgments about who's a better money getter or spender. When it comes to money (like a lot of other things), you're unlikely to create anything new and positive if you're busy making judgments about who your co-spenders and co-earners are.

Here are some questions members of a family might want to ask each other. What are our individual values? Our shared values? How do we connect up these varied values and the money? How do we use our money to create a more developmental environment? Decide, given your value differences, what you want to do about money (and how you want to do it). Then you and your money-sharers can choose what to do with the money rather than the money determining what and who you are. Money, after all, may make the world go 'round. But it's people, with our infinitely varied values, who make the money go 'round.

EXERCISE:

You may find this helps you to see the difference between money and value.

Spend a lot more money than you usually do on something, or someone, you really value but tend not to spend money on.

14

Who Do You Think You Are?

The reigniting of personal development often begins by standing in front of a "mirror" (which could be your social therapy group, a bunch of good friends, a church group or the people you're closest to in your family) and discovering who you really are. This activity of discovery, independent of what we discover, is itself developmental; we change by virtue of engaging in it.

Now wait a second, you may be thinking. *Isn't who we are just… who we are?* Well, yes. But who is that? How we were brought up is certainly part of who we are. So, no doubt, is our genetically passed on physicochemical make-up. So too is what we did last week, and so is what we ate for breakfast this morning. Of course, not every factor is equal — some things are more who we are, and some things are less. Moreover, even though we aren't simply who we think we are, how we think of who we are is an important part of who we are.

Can we change who we are, in general? And, in particular, can we change how we think about who we are? I think we can.

Margaret is a 36-year-old woman from a working class background who "made it" by becoming a lawyer. She is very ambitious, very competitive, and very bright. One night she talked in her social therapy group about the emotional impact of having her beliefs about herself constantly challenged: "I've been so shaken up by what we've been talking about here," she told the group. "I feel like I'm being shaken up at the very core. I get really upset about it. I realize that I can't stand not being completely self-assured."

My response to hearing that Margaret had been "shaken up at the very core" was to say, "Oh! Maybe we can help you get rid of the core altogether, and then perhaps you won't be shaken up anymore at all!" That's one thing we're trying to help people do…to get rid of the core, that individuated self which is forever demanding that it be kept assured and reassured, that individuated identity which is continually in crisis.

But wait a minute, you may say. *Isn't it dangerous, even unnatural (or at least exceedingly difficult) to get rid of it?* I don't believe so — any more than it's dangerous or unnatural or impossibly difficult to remove someone's appendix these days. Just as that useless and often troublesome little tube is a relic from some much earlier period in the biological past of our species, the individuated self — the exaggerated sense of personal identity, along with the myth that having one is what reassures us — is, I believe, an anachronism left over from our more recent societal past. Arguably, it has never been all that useful to the great majority of the earth's people. The individuated self has served the ideological purposes of those 19th century "captains of industry," whose financial and political interests benefited from the division of human consciousness into myriad individuated "selves." Freudian psychology, supposedly a "scientific theory" which described and explained the mental "laws" of this societal invention (the individuated self), emerged in the early years of this century as a model — what I would call a myth. Its glorification of the individual over the group has contributed mightily to economic and societal growth. What it has done to human growth is another matter.

Now all of this isn't to say that the individuated self is so easy to get rid of; it's been at the heart (the core!) of our knowledge, and of our mental, cultural, and political language, for over 300 years. Margaret says that she feels shaken to the very core. What does that mean? What is she saying when she says that? And does it help her out to get rid of that core?

You might not think so. Holding on to the core (her individuated self identity) is, to Margaret's way of thinking, the solution to the problem of her "insecurity." She feels that she'll have nothing left to hold on to if she gives up her most fundamental methodological beliefs — for example, her belief in Problems and Solutions and Explanations and Insights. What she was upset about to begin with was not having enough core, so to speak — that's what Margaret means by "shaken to the core" — and now I want to help her get rid of that, too! Not surprisingly, Margaret has a hard time with this. She understands the desirability of giving up this or that particular deep belief or attitude, and she's smart enough to figure out how to do it. But she's reluctant to give up the core — her individuated self identity — altogether. Yet that's exactly what we need to help her to do.

From a social therapeutic point of view, it's most important that people come to see the difference between who they are and how they think about who they are.

Most of us see ourselves through the lens of society's institutions. Not only what we know about ourselves, but how we know it, is contained in the answers to the questions on the seemingly endless forms modern society requires us to fill out. Your birth certificate gives the date and the place that you were born, your race, your sex. Your old report cards and those forbidding "permanent record cards" say that you "worked and played well with others" when you were six, and that you were a good speller when you were 10. Your driver's license describes the color of your hair and eyes. Your health insurance application states your height and weight and age. Your voter registration card shows your address and your party (ideological) affiliation. Your income tax form tells how much money you make and the names of your "dependents." And so on and on — and on.

In this way people are defined, and define themselves, in terms of the static societal categories, roles, and rule-governed behaviors — their "identity" — which may be useful in all kinds of ways to government bureaucrats, police officials and insurance company executives. But societal identity very much prevents people from knowing themselves as who they are historically. From the vantage point of history, human beings are the active creators and producers of our lives. This is a way of being and living that's at least as important to who we are as our societally defined identity, but it's not so easily labeled or identified or researched.

I believe that the societally biased and bureaucratized distortion of who people are stands in the way of, and eventually stops, human development. In fact, the misunderstanding of who we are historically is what underdevelopment really is. This is different from simply not understanding who we are societally, as children don't, which is what it is to be undeveloped.

Unlike traditional therapy, which tries to resolve "identity crises" by reconstructing and restoring people's sense of identity, the social therapeutic approach works to overcome it and in that way to reinitiate development. Social therapy helps people to know themselves historically — that is, without identity.

Is it possible for human beings to know ourselves in that way? Well, little children, it seems to me, understand very well what things are, and what they themselves are, without identifying or labeling.

What I am calling historical understanding is prevalent in early childhood, when we have a clear sense of our activity as players (without knowing that that's what we are). We create the rules in the activity of playing rather than playing by them. Our sense of ourselves at this early moment of learning and development is far more seamless and far more social than it becomes only a few years later. It is much less encumbered by the constraints of societal categories, which even slightly older children are required to learn: "I'm a boy, I have to…," "I'm too young, I can't…," "I'm not pretty enough to…," "I'm too good for…"

What very young children understand emerges more directly from their social activity; it's not the alienated knowledge based on "information" that comes to predominate once we're even a little bit older and significantly more individuated. It's rather like the distinction between learning to speak our native language (which usually comes early, easily and socially), and learning the grammar and vocabulary of this language (which typically comes later and, for many people, is much, much harder and more individualistic).

When people say "That's just who I am, or how I am…I can't help it," they unintentionally distort the actual process by which human beings live. That distortion is aided by memory, which is often shaped by other people's labeling of us — the "signposts" that tell us what category of person we are: "I was 'the smart one' in the family," "I always had a bad temper," "I could never hold my liquor." The fact is that we are capable of choosing to perform, or not to perform, the roles in which we've been cast. Furthermore, we don't have to perform them according to the way they've been written, and often we don't — people violate the script and "upstage" those roles all the time. We're always making choices, even when we're choosing not to make choices, about how we live.

What the social therapeutic approach takes to be the essential, defining characteristic of humanness is this capacity to make choices, to transform totalities, to see things differently, and to create and recreate our lives even as we are living them. Are we shaped by our biology? No question about it: we are without wings, and so we're unable to fly on our own. Are we formed by society? Clearly: the language we speak, at least at first, is our "mother tongue."

But we are unlike any other species in that we have the capacity to choose, to organize and reorganize culture — to alter the experience of experience itself. No other species, so far as anyone can tell, can do this; while bears and boll weevils may be changed, or change things, they cannot change as a result of their own conscious activity. Neither anteaters nor zebras, nor anything else in between, can choose to live differently. Only human beings can, and do.

What's more, this isn't just true on a large scale, of our species over millennia; it's equally true for each of us hour to hour, moment to moment. It's possible — I would even argue natural — for every human being to lead a life of unlimited, continuous growth and development.

Natural? Yes! While most people tend to be conservative within the context of society, in history people are more naturally radical. Society produces social (not necessarily political) conservatives — people who play by the rules; history produces social (not necessarily political) radicals — people who create something new in the activity of playing. We are, of course, all both — conservative and radical — since we are all both societal and historical. Very young children, who live primarily in history (they haven't yet adapted to society), display their radicalness all the time. It is only to the extent that we stay located in history (although not out of society) that we can continue to grow. If we live exclusively in society, all we can do is adapt by becoming better and better getters.

As people age, they often (although not always and not necessarily) become increasingly attached to, or over-identified with, societal rules. In doing so, ironically, they make themselves more easily definable as "old" — a societal category which, in our culture, has primarily negative associations and consequences.

Age — just like time itself, by which it is conventionally measured — may be useful for administrative purposes, but as with all the other societal categories it sharply limits the possibilities for human growth. Attach some chronological label or identity tag to a human being — "teenager," "middle-aged," "senior citizen" — and you've determined everything from what they should wear, to how they should walk and talk, to how often they should have sex and with whom.

The funny thing is that while age seems absolutely "objective" — simply a matter of fact, like whether you were born on May 12, 1944 or January 8, 1917 or March 17, 1994 — this superimposition of seconds, minutes, hours, days, weeks, months, years, decades and centuries onto the seamless totality of life is actually quite arbitrary. And it's inextricably connected to the equally arbitrary societal construction of the individuated self. Isn't it just as true to say that we're all three billion years old, which is when life began on earth, or a million years old, which is when when *homo sapiens* came on the scene? From that vantage point, the commonality among all of us heavily outweighs the trivial differences between those of us who are in our twenties and those in our seventies or eighties.

But in our Western culture, it's the individualistic differences that are made to count for so much. Aging is related to as taking us nearer and nearer to the precipice of death. This is at least slightly odd, since death is the normal state of affairs; from the vantage point of the human species, someone of 85 is not discernibly nearer to it than someone of 25. So we live "for the moment" (even if that moment was in the past) — as the passive, alienated consumers of time rather than as the active co-producers of history.

When you stop to think about it, it's obvious that most of history is made without us — before we arrive and after we leave. Each of us is "here" for a relatively brief moment. So why should "I" be so presumptuous (self-centered) as to construct my religions and my science and my psychology from "my" point of view?

In social therapy, we don't regard "me" as insignificant — quite the contrary. We simply don't define significance in terms of "me"; we don't take "me" to be the measure of all things. It's not a moral issue; too much me-ness, like cholesterol, just ain't healthy for ya.

EXERCISE:

Try looking at who you are from another point of view.

Have a "we" day — Whenever you ordinarily would start a sentence with "I," change it to "we" and see how that impacts on your day.

15

Breaking Out of Breaking Up

Peter and Barbara had been seeing each other for a little over a year when Peter began talking about their relationship in his social therapy group. He did it reluctantly, having been brought up to believe that such things should be "private." He was even more embarrassed because he felt that what was going on showed him "in a bad light."

Peter and Barbara met when he got a job at the cancer research lab where she had been working for several years. In the beginning, when they were part of the same team, they had a wonderful time. He was eager to learn whatever she could teach him, which she was glad to do; she loved his enthusiasm for the work and his warmth toward her. They fell in love and were soon spending most of their time with one another.

At some point, Peter told us, he started to feel restless in the relationship and, without saying anything, became distant and reserved; Barbara demanded to know what was going on. Finally, Peter told her that he wanted to make new friends and, as a part of that, to be free to date other women. Barbara, angry and hurt, said that she would stop seeing him if he went out with anyone else. Peter backed down, and since then there's been an unspoken agreement between them to avoid the subject of "other women."

I thought that Peter and Barbara needed to have a good look at what they had built together, seeing it in relation to everything else that was going on in their lives, so they could decide where they wanted to go from here.

And I thought it would help to perform that activity of looking "backward" (into their "mirror") in the company of, and with the help of, their closest friends. Indeed, I often suggest that people learn to live their lives "backward" — not obsessively focused on the "future," where there's nothing to see (because, as I say in a philosophically joking way, "there isn't anything there"). Living life backward gives people the opportunity to reshape and reorganize everything that there is, to make something (especially themselves) anew continuously.

Why do Peter and Barbara need their friends to help them see? Because couples, even ones which haven't been together for very long, often tend to resemble fortresses in our culture: two people lock themselves up inside their relationship, rarely getting to see the light of day or to breathe fresh air. And no one else is allowed to see them, except during visiting hours — "official" occasions when they're on their best behavior. The couple, in our culture, is virtually a sacred institution. Other people aren't supposed to know what goes on behind the walls of their relationship.

One consequence of being isolated in this way is that people in couples often tend, eventually, to feel stifled. The couple environment, which is based on a kind of emotional scarcity model (they're only supposed to "have" and "get from" each other, at least emotionally), makes them emotionally undernourished — and, frequently, non-nourishing of the other people in their lives.

Sooner or later, typically, one of the people in a couple starts to experience the very real limits to growth in this situation and tries to end the "sentence" — if not by breaking up, at least by breaking out. If you have any doubts, check out America's divorce rates — not to mention the "affair" rates.

More often than not, when the couple is the man-woman kind, it's the man who's the first to say he wants out. Which is what you'd expect.

For one thing, most women are better than men at growing. Why? They're less overdetermined by the societal requirement to compete than men are, so they're better at asking for help. And they're less invested in appearing to "know it all" beforehand, so they're more willing to do the kind of learning that leads development by doing what they don't know how to do.

For another thing, women tend to be more reluctant than men are to go it alone. Why? Unlike men, who are brought up to be go-getters, women are still brought up primarily to get "a man" — which requires them to be giving only to one person at a time. Once they've got a man, they can be giving to him and to their children, but that's pretty much it. In our culture, women who are "too" giving, to "too many" people (men in particular), sexually speaking and otherwise, get called dirty names. So women tend to think small, within the boundaries of the couple and the family. Men are more worldly; they think bigger — even if they're likely to think that the world revolves around them (or that it should).

Although the institution of the couple keeps both men and women locked in, the societally induced narrowness of women's vision often keeps them from noticing that they're enclosed. Like Barbara, they're likely to resist any suggestion to open the windows and unlock the doors — especially because the "suggestion," when it comes from the man involved, often takes an abusive, blaming, arrogant and selfish form. Men aren't usually very good at saying they want to continue to grow without making it seem like it's the woman's fault that they're not. Often they use other women, or the possibility of other women, to say it. And more often than not, women respond defensively, viewing the man's desire to grow as a threat to the relationship-as-they-know-it (which it is).

But while such endings may be terribly messy for everyone concerned, and often cause women in particular a great deal of pain, I think they're both necessary and positive. Because when a relationship isn't an environment for growth — and I believe that the couple-as-prison, the couple alone together in solitary confinement, does not characteristically encourage growth — it's not just neutral. It's both deadening and deadly. It inevitably falls apart, whether the people involved formally put an end to it or not. And if they don't, they often sit there waiting for the other shoe to fall. Not a happy way to live.

From a social therapeutic standpoint, the relationships that work best are the ones that are intimately interconnected with other people and other life activities. They don't exist as things (couples)-in-themselves, for their own sake; they're not the be-all and end-all of existence for the people in them. The most important question to ask about a relationship is this: is it an environment that supports the growth and development of both of you — not only in the relationship, but in the world?

How do you create such a relationship? By building an environment where both of you are supported to do what you don't know how to do. That's the building activity. One of the primary building materials is what I call radical acceptance — not judgments, a sense of obligation or gratitude, or societal rules. Radical acceptance is a knowing and embracing of who the other person is, which you only get to do in the process of building something together. It means knowing each other in history (in the world), where human beings are their most creative selves. When you have that kind of relationship, you've got something quite special.

And one of the most marvelous things about it is that you don't need to keep it to yourselves. Because the relationship is not so much "having" something as it is doing something.

In a session I did with Barbara and Peter, Barbara said she feels like they're both "walking on eggshells." What are they afraid of? "It's like we're waiting for the end," Peter told me. Like many people in our culture, Peter and Barbara tend to be overdetermined by deadly endings; why else would they be living their lives "waiting for the end" — of anything?

In this situation — when a man says he wants to go out with other women — the societal script calls for the woman in his life to say "The End." But Barbara doesn't necessarily have to close everything down; she can open things up by asking: Where do we go from here? It's actually a very, very common life situation. You start out in the morning on your way to a picnic that you've been planning for two weeks. Then you hear the crash of thunder, you see the flash of lightning, and the rain comes pouring down. The weatherman thinks it won't let up until much later. You can have a tantrum and say: It's all over. The day has been spoiled. Let's go home. Or you can say: Okay. It's raining. What do we do now? You might decide to go home. But you don't have to assume that it's all over just because something has changed. Maybe, after reevaluating the situation, you'll decide to go to the movies or visit a museum you haven't been to for 25 years.

Radical acceptance is the precondition for engaging in this kind of activity in a way that's not destructive: let whatever the other person says and does influence the direction that you go in, and see where that takes you. Rather than doing what you're supposed to do in a conversation, which is to wait your turn and then say what you want to say or where you want to go, your response can be: Hmmm. Well, I never thought of going there. Let's try it. You'll find there are all kinds of interesting places to go, emotionally and physically, if you allow yourself to be led — not by the nose, but by your own choice.

So instead of jumping to an ending conclusion — Barbara's knee-jerk, judgmental reaction to what Peter is saying — she could take this opportunity to see how she and Peter can use what's happening to develop. That's the starting point. She could say: We seem to want different things right now. We could go down different paths. But that's not the only thing we can do.

Why is it so unusual for people in couples to talk that way to one another? I think it's difficult to practice radical acceptance if all you have is the two of you. In this situation, Barbara is clinging to the relationship-as-it-is as if that's all that she can expect to have. Her self-degrading, deprivational, culture-of-getting assumption is that she can't grow — so why should Peter be allowed to?

A guiding principle of many couples within the societal institution of coupledom is that both partners are primarily dedicated to the couple. Their deepest emotional aspirations and desires are supposed to be achieved and satisfied within it. The "point" of the couple, from this vantage point, is its own perpetuation. Its success is often measured by the length of time that two people have been together, and only secondarily, or not at all, by what and how well they do together. We celebrate anniversaries of calendar years, not quality years! The fundamental commitment is to having things remain the way they've "always" been — which means that you throw out whatever's dissonant with that. In this kind of conservative relationship, the promise that the partners make to each other (whether that takes the form of marriage vows or is simply an unspoken "understanding") is: I will forever be the way I am now.

From the social therapeutic point of view, it's qualitative activity (not quantitative duration) that matters; the most important question to ask about a couple is whether it's an environment in which development is supported — where both people can grow. Such an environment, of course, entails a risk, which is that one or both partners might grow in ways which lead them to want to do things that aren't consistent with perpetuating the couple. It can certainly be very painful, and very sad, when that happens.

But it's not possible to create an environment which is growthful and, at the same time, insist that a condition for participating in that environment is that neither of you can grow! In other words, it doesn't make sense to be judgmental because someone has grown in an environment that supports growth.

Look at it this way: if you set up a painting school, you run the risk that someone might come along who learns to paint much better than you do. You can't be angry about it; that's the risk you take with a painting school which is even halfway good. The risk is that if you build an environment worth building, it might impact on you.

In a growthful relationship, the fundamental commitment is to development; radical acceptance means that you take whatever comes along and see how you both can use it to grow. The promise that the partners make (if they choose to make one) is not that things will be the same forever, but that they will always be there for each other, whatever happens.

In any given social therapy group, for example, there are always some people who work as hard as they can to create the environment — and other people who hang out in the group, take what's been built and use it to get something for themselves somewhere else. They're perfectly within their "rights" to do that, of course. (They're paying — even if, in my opinion, they don't get their money's worth with this "rip-off" strategy.) But the activity of creating the environment goes on because there are still people there who want to do that work.

When one person leaves a couple, however, there's no one left to build "the group" because there's no "group" left. That's why the practice of radical acceptance is much more "at home" in an environment that's broad enough to include other people. If one of the partners in a couple decides to go somewhere or do something else for a while, the other person isn't left alone, emotionally speaking.

Certainly, it's possible for someone to give her or his "all" to more than one emotional environment. But in my experience, most people are some combination of unwilling and unable to do that; if they're here, then they won't or can't be there. I'm not just referring to sexual relationships, by the way — people who are deeply involved in their work tend to want to come home and chill out, without giving very much to the people they live with. So when someone says, as Peter is saying to Barbara, that he wants to see other women but that he's still committed to having the relationship with her, I think she has to be prepared for him not to be there for her. In this kind of situation, other emotionally friendly environments are invaluable.

Many people, not surprisingly, are particularly incompetent at doing endings. I say "not surprisingly," because the societal experience of loss that goes with endings in our culture can be so profound.

Suddenly, or so it may seem, your property has to be divided: the cat you adopted together, the wine glasses you bought at a yard sale, your favorite tapes, a big old sweater that you took turns wearing. You've got the feeling that life won't be the same. (It won't). Suddenly, there's no one to do with you the things you've·"always done" together: going to the movies on Saturday nights, celebrating holidays, spending vacations. Suddenly, you no longer have the validation (the societal nod of approval we earn when we can prove we're socially, emotionally and sexually desirable enough) that comes with having someone to go out with, or live with, or be married to. Suddenly, you have to contemplate all the dangers and difficulties entailed in going back out into the arena where the dating game is played.

I think these practical considerations tend to be underestimated. They're often ignored in favor of the romanticized assumption that what makes breaking up so hard to do is the emotional trauma that it causes. Certainly there can be a lot of sadness when a relationship ends, for both people involved — even when one of them is leaving and the other person is being left. But it's also often the case that by the time the end comes, there's not so much intensity of feeling on either person's part.

It rarely happens that everything is absolutely fine for one person in a relationship while the other person is miserable, or even just dissatisfied. Peter, for example, was the first to articulate his "restlessness," but it turned out that Barbara was also — or more — unhappy with the situation. Still (and again, this is not to deny the sadness and the pain), it seems to me that the practical hardships people face when they break up a relationship, a household, or a marriage can be the hardest part.

The trouble with endings is that they tend to be overdetermined by the societal experience of loss. An ending is almost never viewed in a positive light, as an opportunity to grow; it's rarely regarded as being developmental. All too often, people who are ending a relationship become so embittered, so saddened, so despairing, that they wind up throwing away everything that was worthwhile in the relationship (which very much heightens their experience of loss). In denying what they've built together, they negate what's potentially developmental — which stands in the way of their continuing to grow.

In social therapy we work very hard to help people break up, if that's what they choose to do, without negating what they've done and without negating the pain that they are feeling at the moment. (Injections are often painful and they frequently make us better.) It's possible for people to find ways of using everything there is, including the pain, for further development by locating the activity of ending in the broader totality of their life activity. Things end, lovers break up, people age and die — and development doesn't have to stop.

EXERCISES:

Doing this will help you to see what a little radical acceptance can do.

Go a whole day without saying "Yes, but..." once — just say "Yes," and see what difference that makes.

———

This will help you to see the value of reorganizing everything all the time.

For one whole day, reorganize everything every 15 minutes — regardless of whether or not things are going the way you want them to go.

16

Don't Be So Particular

When people have had a very painful or tragic experience in their lives — childhood abuse, the debilitating illness of someone to whom they were close, financial disaster, the failure of a marriage — or if they simply have a generalized and pervasive feeling that they aren't good enough, pretty enough, smart enough, or rich enough to live the kind of life they'd like to live, they often express an understandable desire to be completely rid of those negative experiences or factors. They wish they could be "a whole new person," "wipe the slate clean," "live life over again." Unfortunately, however, the experiences and factors that caused us so much pain as children or as adults tend to stay with us (indeed, they are part of us) — and so do our emotional responses to them: anger, grief, hostility, humiliation, jealousy.

The serious question, from the social therapeutic standpoint, is: given that you have (are) these tragic experiences, negative factors and emotional responses (together with all the other life experiences you've had), can you live your life without being a complete victim of them? Do we have to be victimized by who we are? Can we use the negative experiences and, more generally, the negative factors, to change who we are? Or is one more bad day to be merely another occasion for wishful thinking that the negative experience and the "bad me" had never happened?

In social therapy (unlike most traditional approaches), we do not help people to "work on" the particular feeling that they want to get out (the way Lady Macbeth tried to do — futilely, I must remind you — with her damned spot). From a social therapeutic vantage point, such negative experiences are elements of, and are located within, a total life — a life which must be constantly reorganized and transformed in its totality, because that, in my opinion, is the only way particulars are ever changed. We have to change not some specific feature(s) of ourselves, but how we *are* — and we must do so continuously.

Astonishingly, this is vastly easier than trying to change particulars — and it's easier than you think! While I don't believe that you can be "a whole new person" or that you can "wipe the slate clean" or "live life over again," I do think you can change who you are by radically accepting who you are and using that (you) to continue to develop.

When a woman says that her boss is harassing her sexually, or a man says he has trouble maintaining an erection during sex with his wife, I don't think that the way to deal with each particular "problem" is to "work on" it. Instead, the social therapeutic approach supports people to go beyond the limits imposed by a particular situation, and by the traditional problem-solution way of thinking that comes with it, in order to help them change how they live their whole lives. Changing the totality, not surprisingly, has a profound impact on the particular elements that are part of it. Forget the particular problem. Change YOU.

Here is an example of what I'm talking about. Last year, Gerri was a partner in a small, successful restaurant that she and two of her friends started about 20 years ago. The work was demanding, the hours were long, and Gerri worked harder than anybody else. She told her social therapy group that she had to "take care of everything and everyone." Just for the record, her partners said that Gerri interfered with their work, and that her constant "worrying" came across as a criticism of them.

Gerri's attitude was that if she didn't take care of it, no one would — and that even if they did, they wouldn't do it right (which meant the way she would do it). For years she wouldn't take a vacation, or a day off, for fear that "things would fall apart" without her. She came in even when she was sick.

Gerri told us about the many particular problems at the restaurant: the chef was leaving and they still hadn't found anyone to replace him; the landlord didn't want to renew their lease; she felt overwhelmed with work and responsibility; there was growing tension between her and her partners. Gerri said the situation at work was driving her crazy: "What can I do about it?" she wanted to know.

What could she do about it? Nothing. The "it" of it, the particularity of it, was for the most part impossible to alter in a way that would make a real difference to Gerri. Unfortunately, we have been socialized to believe that it is easier to change smaller things. Not so. What Gerri could change was how she was living her life. She could change the totality. She could reinitiate her development and become someone new. Every "problematic" life situation offers us that wonderful opportunity.

In one social therapy group, I asked Gerri to talk about the totality of her life — forget the problems of the business for a moment and tell us what else is going on. The most important thing in her life, Gerri said, was her relationship with Stephanie, a violinist. Stephanie is highly regarded in the world of classical music, and Gerri was very proud of her accomplishments. It was the second long-term relationship for both and they loved one another deeply; they were closely involved in each other's lives.

Stephanie usually called Gerri two or three times a day at the restaurant: maybe she had some gossip to tell Gerri about her musician friends, or news (a record contract, a favorable review); she would ask Gerri to pick something up from the supermarket on her way home, or she wanted Gerri's opinion about this or that. Stephanie went out of her way to ask what Gerri thought she should do (although Stephanie's actually a better decision-maker than Gerri is), and Gerri stopped whatever she was doing to talk with her. Although neither of them had ever said so aloud, one of Gerri's many "jobs" seemed to be taking care of Stephanie.

When I suggested that Gerri could reorganize her relationship with Stephanie, she was shocked, upset and angry. "No! Why!?" Her relationship with Stephanie, she insisted, was the best thing in her life! Why should she change that?

That's precisely why she needed to reorganize it, I suggested. It's the good things in our lives — the strongest things — that are most reorganizable in the process of transforming our total lives (who we are), because they're least likely to break in the process. When something's strong, you can put more weight on it. You can build a new life on your strengths and, in the process, alter, transform, relocate your weaknesses.

That's why we make it a rule of thumb in social therapy to help people look at how the best things in their lives are organized and urge them (much as they might want to avoid doing so) to take a look at how that might be contributing to what isn't so good: where and how do you see the weaknesses of your life as expressed in the strengths? They are connected, after all — by your life. Although people often talk about their "problems" as if everything else were completely "fine" — "The only thing wrong with me is this isolated thing over here" — weaknesses typically aren't isolated, like socks in a sock drawer. They're pervasive; they "seep through" and get expressed everywhere, in different ways. That's why, when a good coach spots a weakness in his or her team, he or she often looks to see how it's embodied in the team's strongest areas of play and works on it there. By reorganizing the strengths, you impact on the weakness; that's how the team as a whole gets stronger.

In focusing on the strengths and thereby reshaping the totality, you relocate each of the particulars within a broader environment — thereby changing their relationship to each other and to the whole. You create something new out of what there was and, in doing so, you recast or relocate the "problem." The "problem" is thus "eliminated" rather than "solved." This is not a way of avoiding the problem; rather, it is changing your relationship to the problem by transforming what is easiest to change in that relationship: YOU.

This is very different, of course, from traditional Freudian and Freudian-influenced therapy, whose bedrock is the assumption that your past life — which supposedly determines almost completely who you are — is basically unchangeable: YOU cannot be transformed. For example, traditional therapy often tries to help people solve their problematic relationships with their parents by "revisiting" the past, reexamining again and again an area of their lives which is weak — as children, they were dependent and powerless in those relationships. The hope is that this will, however slightly, alter the future...that it will solve the "presenting problem."

The social therapeutic view is based on a very different philosophical understanding. From this perspective, there is no future other than what we human beings personally and collectively create from the materials of the so-called past. The social therapeutic approach helps people not merely to look backward for an insightful, analytical visit. Our philosophical understanding calls for people to live backward (that is, historically) — to change the past in order for there to be a future.

If the past (like our "identity") is unchangeable, then we are truly determined by "it." But in fact the past, like our individuated "identity," is transformable. Think about it in this very practical way: what you say at the end of a sentence characteristically determines the meaning of the beginning of the sentence. The spoken sentence begins in the "past" and ends in the "present." But it is the ending — the completion — which determines the meaning of the beginning (the past). Here's a little language game to help you see: Complete the following sentence in three different ways. I'd like to hold your _____.

In social therapy, we examine how people's relationships in the present embody the weaknesses of the past. Social therapy cures people by helping them to change the present to transform the past. I sometimes like to talk about past and present history as a rope. The so-called present is what we have in our hand, and the so-called past is the rest of the rope. When we wriggle the rope from the "present" end, the "past" changes. To do this we must become wrigglers of life (the rope, the "past") rather than be locked into the deadly identity of the wriggled.

The dialogue with Gerri that I've been telling you about took place over a period of months. For a long time, she was adamant. There was no reason to reorganize her relationship with Stephanie, Gerri insisted, because the restaurant was the problem. Then, during one very emotional group session, she told us: "I'm afraid that if I don't take care of Stephanie she won't stay. I'll be abandoned." Moreover, Gerri thought that was true of all the people in her life — her business partners, her friends, her family. If she didn't "take care of everything," she told us, she was afraid that maybe no one would stay. So she did take care. She was perpetually busy trying to determine the future, rather than working to transform the past (wriggling the rope) — and herself.

The issue for Gerri was not that she had "too much to do," but how she lived her life. She was like a juggler who juggles frantically, whether she's got three balls in the air or 13. Although she took care of Stephanie too much, that hadn't (yet!) become a "problem." At the restaurant it was. But she couldn't do something about *it* — Gerri needed to change who *she* was (her life, her "past," her "identity" as the person who took care of everyone).

Gerri had to see that to do something about the particular situation she wanted to change, she had to look at her entire life so she could see and do something about the particulars in relation to how the totality — her life, her self — was organized.

Eventually she did. She could look at what was strongest in her life — her relationship with Stephanie — and, because she was least defensive there, see the weaknesses in it that she couldn't see elsewhere. What she saw was that she "needed" to take care of everyone in order to make sure that she would be needed, since she didn't think that anyone wanted her. And she decided that she didn't want to live her life like that anymore.

What happened? About a year later, Gerri dumped the business. "The truth is, after 20 years it's become a pain in the neck," she told us. Her relationship with Stephanie grew even stronger when Gerri stopped taking care of her, giving both of them the opportunity to see that Stephanie wanted to be with her and that Gerri didn't have to pay such a price for it.

Now that she no longer feels the need to take care of everyone, Gerri is considering what she wants to do with her life. It's a liberating experience — she can do all kinds of things that she couldn't do before, when what she did was overdetermined by her need to be identified as the caretaker. No longer stuck in that role, Gerri has begun to develop and grow again. She hasn't become "a new person" — but she's continuing to change her life.

EXERCISE:

Here's a way to see what it would be like to change your life.

Think of an area of your life that's strong — that's going well — do it differently for a day, and see how that impacts on your whole life.

17

Here's Looking at You

In our getting culture, physical appearance has a big impact on how we're perceived, which in turn often influences what and how much we're able and unable to get — dates, attention in the shoe store, jobs, and a whole lot more besides. If we appear to be too fat or too old, disabled or disfigured, or if we don't have the right clothes or the right kind of nose, we're more likely to get turned down, ignored or dismissed than those who've got "good looks." Which isn't to say that good-looking people don't also have to deal with other people's competitiveness, which can be expressed in ways that are hurtful and even hostile. But it is a fact of life in our culture that appearances, while they aren't everything, mean a lot.

This is especially (although not only) true for women. A great deal has been written by scholars of varying points of view about the economic and political origins of the subjugation of women (their reduction to the status of property). The institution of marriage (as it came to be sanctified by religion and legitimized by the state) originated millennia ago in the social contract between a woman's family and a man which required that he be given exclusive rights to her sexuality; in return he agreed to provide for and protect her (from nature and from other men), while assuming responsibility for the children he had with her.

There's a very long tradition in our culture (in common with many others) of identifying women as the sexual property of men and, as such, as objects to be adorned. One of the many lingering cultural expressions of women's status as property (which has largely — but not completely — disappeared from the law) is that, at the end of the 20th century, women are still expected to make themselves attractive in order to arouse men's desire. Another cultural remnant of women-as-property is that it is customary for men to use "their" women to display what else they own to other men, which is why men are frequently "invested" in how good "their" women look.

One consequence of all this is that it's not only appropriate, but more or less required, in our culture that women work hard to look good (according to the prevailing societal standards): to dye or bleach the hair on their heads, remove their body and facial hair, pierce their ears, paint their toenails and fingernails, "make up" their faces, and diet to lose weight. Some women even undergo surgery to make their faces and bodies conform to societal models of attractiveness.

Making themselves attractive is one of the ways that women play the getting game. I believe very strongly that women have as much right to play our culture's primary game — the getting game — as men do. As is true when men play it, the game can be played in an endless variety of ways; some are more effective and less self-destructive, while others are ineffective and very self-destructive. I urge that, whoever is playing, the game be played as developmentally as possible.

As you might suspect, women getting good at the getting

game is not the whole story — it never is, because human beings (women and men alike) are not merely cultural products; we're cultural creators. Many, many women have fun with cosmetics and with clothes, using enormous creativity, imagination, wit and daring in doing so. They don't conform, passively, to narrow societal definitions of what it means to look good. Nor are they obedient to the reverse morality of prohibitionistic feminism, which requires them to renounce the cosmetic equivalent of the demon rum if they want to be "saved" from sexism.

Millions of women choose to "make themselves up" for fun, to show their style, to strut their stuff — not simply for the purpose of getting, but more in the spirit of giving. Their "fashion statement" is: I'm doing this not because I have to, but because I want to. It is, in fact, a wonderful way in which women play with other women.

Linda is a very beautiful woman who made up her mind when she was still in high school that it was "too hard" to be beautiful. The boys were always "making remarks" to her, and the girls treated her as a rival who had an unfair advantage, which hurt her. "I couldn't stand it," she told her social therapy group. "I didn't want them to make assumptions about me based on what they saw." Now 36, Linda almost never "dresses up" — she wears bulky sweaters and baggy pants and has a "practical" haircut. Recently a close friend asked Linda if she knew that she was beautiful (Linda said she did) and why she never "showed" anyone her beauty. Linda had never really thought about it like that. "I want to be recognized for my accomplishments, not for what I look like," she said. "What's wrong with that?"

From the social therapeutic standpoint, there isn't anything wrong with what Linda is saying; what I asked was why she was (and whether she wanted to be) committed to letting her appearance determine her life to such an extent. Where was *she* in deciding how she wanted to look? I appreciated her unwillingness to be exploited for her looks, or to use her beauty to exploit other people, I told her. But, given that her extraordinary beauty is something that she has, she could decide, if she chose, what she wanted to do with it. Getting ripped off by men, or ripping other women off, weren't her only two choices. She could decide to give her beauty.

I do not advocate that people stop playing the getting game (what was called in the '60s "tuning in, turning on, dropping out"). I think the issue is how you play (rather than if you should), and whether or not you want your life to be completely determined by it. So, for example, if you're a lawyer you might decide to wear a suit and tie when you appear in court because, if you don't, the judge is likely to have an attitude about your appearance that could adversely affect your client. But sooner or later you have to take that suit off. Then what? What's the relationship between your image (what you look like) and who you are?

Who you are includes and is informed by how you look, which in turn gives expression to who you are. Development is the activity that transforms the totality of who you are, while improving your image has to do with a particular — your appearance. The social therapeutic approach teaches people that their appearance doesn't have to replace them; we support them to let the continuously transforming totality of who they are take precedence in defining how they look.

I've always been a slow jogger — I've been doing 15-minute miles since I was in my thirties. At 35, that wasn't too impressive. But my plan is to keep on doing 15-minute miles. As I see it, by the time I'm 100 it'll be sensational!

Yes, the point I'm making, once again, is that we need to focus on totalities rather than particulars. There is the totality of life as we're living it at a given moment, rather than the particular aspect of life that has to do with how we look. And there's the totality of a whole lifetime, rather than the particular moment during it when we're supposed to be "at our most attractive."

In other words, how you live your life to look stunning at 25 may be very different from how you live at that age if you want to look good all your life. You can make conscious decisions about how you want to look and what you want to do to look that way in the context of deciding how you want to live your whole life.

This is the same kind of choice people make, by the way, when they're deciding whether they want to bring up their children in order to maximize what they get out of being the parents of adorable, clever six-year-olds, or to maximize what they can give to youngsters to enable them to live satisfying and productive lives when they're 30, 40, and 50.

When the focus is on the totality of life, you can decide to look stunning without having to be concerned about becoming over-identified with that one aspect of who you are — your looks would be a part of the totality. In the absence of such a total life plan, some very beautiful people hide their beauty for fear of having that become the totality of who they are — and end up being humiliated by it, as we are by whatever aspect of ourselves that we keep hidden.

The following excerpt from a recent article on cellulite ("the dreaded orange-peel effect") in the "Beauty" section of a well known fashion magazine for women will sound familiar to anyone who has ever taken a clinical interest in sado-masochism. Written only slightly tongue-in-cheek, the article describes the author's experience with an expensive technique called cellulopolysis, "a new wonder treatment" from France:

"...the prospect of a lifetime with a pair of dimply thighs was even more horrifying than having electric currents pumped through my legs...I would embrace the electric chair if it got rid of cellulite...[In the first session] it took about half an hour to insert all [eight] needles and wire them up to the machine next to the bed...[The nurse] handed me a gadget that controls the amount of electricity entering each needle and I became my own torturer. The electricity stimulates the area around the needles, to improve circulation, kick-start the metabolism and flush out the waste, fat and toxins that cause cellulite...I have lost three centimetres from my thighs. I weigh ten pounds less than at the start and the dimpling that's left is kind of subtle...I shall be wearing a bikini this summer, and the news hasn't made my husband nervous."

What's wrong with this picture?

From a social therapeutic point of view, being in good shape — fit and healthy — is most likely to be lasting and genuine when it's produced by who you are. That's very different from appearing as the image of what a bathing suit designer or a nutritionist or the "Beauty" editor says you ought to look like. While looking good is often a product of development, in my experience it rarely produces development.

Which is why, in my view, exercising very often "works" and dieting hardly ever does. If you're looking good but not having a good and developmental time doing what you have to do to look that way, what you're doing isn't likely to last. Dieting, it seems to me, is essentially punitive; it's designed to deprive people who have committed the sin of "self-indulgence" (otherwise known as "overeating") of the pleasure and gratification that come from eating and drinking things we enjoy. Advocates of dieting prey on people's shame and humiliation about our bodies, and on our guilty way of seeing and thinking in response to other people's real or imagined judgments about what and how much we eat.

The underlying assumption of diets is that "fat" people are "addicted" to food in general, or certain foods in particular. The thinking (I'm being generous in describing it as such) goes that for some reason, which varies from diet theory to diet theory, and from year to year, some of us "can't handle" carbohydrates, or fats, or sugar, so we should only be allowed to have them in extremely limited amounts or not at all. Not surprisingly, dieting — the "solution" to the false "problem" of "addictive" eating — is highly ineffective. People go through a deprivational, punitive, negating experience which is often extremely painful and in many (if not most) cases end up in the same position as when they started.

There is, of course, all the difference in the world between dieting and changing what and how you eat. Changing how we eat is one way of continuously transforming ourselves developmentally. If you want to transform who you are physically, then in my opinion it's better in every way to initiate that process by exercising rather than by dieting.

In saying this, I'm not trying to turn exercising into The Right Thing To Do, a Way of Life or any other kind of Authorized Activity. It's simply that dieting is anti-developmental in its essence. Exercising is all about development.

To begin with, exercising is a positive activity which changes your relationship to your body from the moment that you lift your first weight, swim your first lap, take your first aerobic deep breath or move your arms like a cross country skier. You are literally giving positive shape to your total body. I believe that exercise tends to work (while diets tend not to work) not primarily because it burns up calories, but because exercise allows us to give physical expression to who we are. While dieting almost never impacts on exercise, when people exercise it almost always, in my experience, affects their eating patterns.

Unlike dieting, which is a highly individuated and often isolating activity, exercising is much more naturally social. And regardless of why you're lifting weights, swimming, jumping up and down in time to a Calypso beat or cross country skiing in your bedroom, it can be fun in and of itself. I don't think anyone who's ever dieted can say the same for going without foods they enjoy.

One of the things I like best about exercising is that you don't have to wait to be the person you want to become — as soon as you start exercising, you're doing (in some manner, shape or form) what the person you'd most like to look like is doing.

Having said all of this, I'm aware that there may be some of you who believe that, in your case, it's still a matter of "do or die-t." If you do, here's a small slice of advice. Go on what the diet folks call "maintenance" right away — start out by eating how you want to be eating at the end of the diet and for the rest of your life!

From the standpoint of social therapy (which is, as you've seen by now, a "no-step" approach), it makes much more sense to live your life fully now as the 120-pound person you want to be than to deprive yourself for three months or six months or a year for the sake of the future (probably non-existent) 120-pound person you'll be someday. Even according to the logic of dieting itself, it makes more sense. Many, many diets fail at the maintenance stage. So I say: Begin there! And while it may take you a little bit longer, it's healthier, in my opinion, in every way. Try it. After all, what have you got to lose?

EXERCISE:

You can invent your own.

Devise a five-minute physical exercise — maybe breathing, or stretching — that you can handle. Do it (without overdoing it) every day for a week and see what it does for you.

18

Warning on the Label: This Treatment May Be Dangerous To Your Development

"Hyperactive." "Learning disabled." "Emotionally disturbed." "Developmentally delayed." "Slow." "Impaired." These are among the labels that special education, an offshoot of the pseudoscience of psychology, attaches to millions of children who, for one reason or another, get into trouble with the adults responsible for them. Such labels are a description (a diagnosis of the "problem"), and they imply a prescription (the "solution," which usually includes drugs). There is a growing recognition, by the way, among many parents and educators that "special ed" is a tragic failure for the vast majority of children involved in it.

Do some kids do better on certain kinds of tests than other kids do? Undoubtedly. Is it possible to assign a number to those differences? Yes, and then you can talk about who is "normal," who is "gifted," who is "retarded" and who is "borderline." Whatever the numbers, and whatever the labels that go with them, this activity puts children on a track which is unlikely to take them in a developmental direction. The full weight of "science" is often behind that description/prescription of the label, making it extremely difficult for kids to get out from under it — to take another road.

It isn't that classifying symptoms, in and of itself, is necessarily a bad thing to do. For example, it's very helpful to people to be told that their physical symptoms indicate that they're diabetic, or anemic, or that they have a heart condition, and to have this confirmed by the results of laboratory tests or x-rays. Once you and your doctors know what disease you've got, you and they can begin to treat it.

But when it comes to the classification of psychological symptoms and administering psychological tests which supposedly prove that a child has "got" some emotional or cognitive disease or condition, we run the risk that the symptom-based label the "experts" come up with will overdetermine the treatment. The danger is that the treatment will focus exclusively on dealing with — eliminating or masking — the symptoms while ignoring the child's emotional and cognitive development. The application by psychologists of a pseudo-medical model that imposes labels — and, often, drugs — on children who are "difficult" short-circuits the possibility that they can be helped to grow and develop further.

Classification and labeling are part of a paradigm, a way of seeing, that has been highly useful to the physical sciences in dealing with the natural world. Over the past hundred years or so, medicine has borrowed that model and often put it to very good use. Think of the great discoveries and inventions in medicine as a whole, and in surgery and chemical therapy in particular, that have vastly improved the quality of life for millions and millions of people. But it doesn't automatically follow from those achievements that the model is applicable to emotional and intellectual development. In fact, this hand-me-down approach by psychology has been, in my opinion, of doubtful benefit to the very people — adults as well as children — clinical psychology seeks to help. It's simply not relevant to us as thinking, feeling beings. Of course, the psychological "experts" who get money, grants, tenure, and credibility for classifying and labeling the rest of us are an exception; it's very relevant, and profitable, for them.

Jay is a man in his early thirties who grew up very poor, and was seemingly headed for utter failure. When he was eight years old, he had what was diagnosed as an epileptic seizure and was given medication for it which he continued to take until very recently. He had also been on anti-depressants since childhood. Jay came into social therapy a few years ago. During that time, he's earned a master's degree in biology and begun applying to medical schools. Several weeks ago he told his social therapy group that he's decided to stop taking medication. "If I have a seizure, I can handle it," he said. "I have the resources to deal with the consequences, so I can choose what I want to do." In social therapy, Jay learned how to create his own life — how to develop.

The social therapeutic approach is not anti-drug as a moral position. However, we don't accept the currently hip, faddish presupposition that people are fundamentally biochemical or that their "problems" are reducible to biochemistry. If you view people as essentially biochemical in nature, then you will "naturally" come up with biochemical remedies to deal with their "problems." But human beings are not reducible to our biology or our chemistry (although, to be sure, who we are includes our biological and chemical processes).

It's certainly possible to find drugs that will impact on schizophrenia, depression, hyperactivity and all sorts of other mental and emotional illnesses. If you put powerful chemicals into people's bodies, they will undoubtedly be affected by it. Yes, it might mute or even do away with unpleasant or disruptive symptoms. Indeed, it might even be exactly what's needed!

My question is: does that treatment impede development? Isn't it possible that treating the symptoms with drugs may simultaneously stigmatize the people who are being "helped" and be used (however unjustifiably) to justify mistreating them? Isn't it possible that, in this way, the door to a more effective, broader, developmental treatment of their illness is being closed to them? Does taking high-powered drugs to alleviate symptoms effectively deny human responsibility and choice, which are critical to continued development?

In other words, is taking drugs to deal with mental and emotional illness a passive reaction to symptoms that reduces the likelihood of discovering ways to get help which are truly developmental? Is the price that people end up paying for getting "help" with their symptoms the closing off of their capacity for unlimited development?

I take aspirin when I have a headache, so I would never suggest that people who are in far greater pain should not have access to drugs. To say that would be not only hypocritical; it would be inhuman. But it's even more hypocritical, and more inhuman, in my opinion, to relegate people to a lifetime of drug taking at the price of their potential development — and to argue for doing so on the grounds that it makes them more manageable. From a social therapeutic perspective, if helping professionals are going to medicate people, then the drugs have to be part of an overall plan to reinitiate development. If they're only willing or able to deal with symptoms, they're engaged not in a "helping" activity but in social control.

From the vantage point of social therapy, if a treatment form is inconsistent with development then it's seriously problematic. In other words, in order to judge the effectiveness of any approach you have to know what its relationship is to continuous human development — your own, and the development of the people you care for. The "experts" tell you a particular treatment will be helpful. But what's the cost? Will it impair your capacity to grow? The child psychiatrist or the school psychologist tells you that your kid is "hyperactive" and needs to take Ritalin once or twice a day for the rest of his life. You've got to say: "Ritalin and what else? I want something that will help my child. I'll take the Ritalin, but not as a substitute for development. If you're telling me you've got Ritalin and nothing else, you're telling me to give up on my child. And that's not acceptable to me."

We have to ask the development question *every* time, in *every* situation. (When you're about to get into bed with someone you like, you need to say something like: "This looks like it might be a lot of fun, and I would love to do it. How will it affect your development, and mine?")

Social therapy helps people to deal with their lives — including mental and emotional illness — without the labeling (and everything that goes with it) which limits their capacity to develop further. We have discovered that concentrating on development, not "problems," is what helps people most and most immediately. In other words, we have found that development is what's curative.

Development is not an abstraction, but an activity; it is something that people decide to do. The essence of the social therapeutic approach is that, from the very beginning, we relate to people — and teach them to relate to themselves and one another — on the basis of their strengths and not on the basis of their symptoms (whatever they may be).

In contrast to our "friends" the diet "experts," the unofficial motto of social therapy is: Start with maintenance. Just as I think that people should, from the very beginning, eat as much as they're "allowed" to when they reach their "ideal" weight (thus bypassing the stage of punitive deprivation known as "dieting"), the social therapeutic approach bypasses the punitive, humiliating and often very long-lasting stage in traditional therapy when people are related to and defined by their symptoms and labels and, in many cases, by their treatment. That's what I mean by saying that social therapy is a "no-step" approach.

I hereby issue this challenge to any psychiatrist of any "school":

You can have five minutes each with 12 patients and prescribe whatever medication you think appropriate for their symptoms. I'll do a one-hour social therapy group with those same 12 patients. I believe that, whatever their labels, they'll have a better life for the next four or five days following that one hour than they will during the time that the drugs are in effect — presumably about four or five days. Social therapy simply works better than drugs. Development, in my experience, is more effective than sedation.

EXERCISE:

Try this experiment the next time you have a headache or a hangover (or just a bad day).

Give social expression to what's bothering you — talk to someone you wouldn't ordinarily talk to about it — and see what effect that has.

19

Anxiety, Panic, and Worry

Anxiety is an important concept in the vocabulary of the pseudo-science of psychology. According to the "Glossary of Technical Terms" in the third edition of the *Diagnostic and Statistical Manual of Mental Disorders* published by the American Psychiatric Association (the official authority on such subjects), anxiety "...stems from the anticipation of danger, which may be internal or external. Some definitions of anxiety distinguish it from fear by limiting it to the anticipation of danger, the source of which is largely unknown...It may be experienced in discrete periods of sudden onset and be accompanied by physical symptoms (panic attacks)."

"Panic" and "anxiety" are not merely part of the official lingo; they're also household words that describe very common experiences in the everyday lives of millions of people. From a social therapeutic perspective, panic and anxiety are best understood in terms of the unique societal arrangements that produce them.

As I see it, anxiety is an emotion that goes rather well with the culture of getting. What's "unknown" is whether you're going to get all you want; people feel anxious day and night about whether they're getting enough, getting it right, getting what they deserve, getting ahead, and all the other variations on the getting theme. Anxiety, in my view, is an experience of fear which is usually connected to a very specific situation — although with a generalized foreboding that you're not "getting it" or that you won't "get it." It can often act as a spur to productive activity — asking for a raise, making a phone call, writing a paper, announcing that you're leaving. As long as our culture is organized around the getting principle, I think it's probably futile to try to get rid of anxiety altogether. But that's not to say that we're doomed to be the passive victims of it. Rather, we need to create our own anxieties — to decide what we want to get, and how to be better getters given who we are and what we believe in.

Panic, on the other hand, although it is also societally produced, is nevertheless an emotion of another color. This is how Robert and Deirdre talked about their "panic attacks" in their social therapy group.

Robert leaves his office to go to lunch. He's walking down the street and suddenly he breaks into a cold sweat, his heart pounding. He feels as if he's choking and he's filled with dread.

The same thing happens to Deirdre. The kids are at school, her husband is at work, she's cooking or straightening up the house. Then — boom! "Out of the blue" she becomes paralyzed with fear.

Neither Robert nor Deirdre knows of any reason for these episodes — nothing is very wrong in either of their lives. Deirdre, who's 30, has had such attacks three or four times a year since she was a teenager; they usually last a few hours, leaving her exhausted and shaken. Robert, who's in his forties, just started having them two or three years ago; the most recent one lasted for several weeks, during which he was hospitalized for a nervous breakdown.

Unlike anxiety, it seems to me, panic has no socially "redeeming" qualities; since it often takes the form of paralysis, it can hardly be used to produce development. Nor does it get you anything. What causes panic is literally nothing — the experience of nothingness and meaninglessness that is, arguably, a unique characteristic of our postmodern culture. It's not just that there's "nothing to be afraid of," as the experts suggest about anxiety; when people like Robert and Deirdre panic, they're responding to the fact that there is (or seems to be) nothing, period.

However fearful human beings may have been in other moments and times, they always knew — or thought they knew — what they were afraid of: the gods' wrath, marauding animals, other people. And they knew what they had to rely on: prayer and sacrifice, weapons, war. In our postmodern culture, we feel ourselves standing on shaky societal ground with nothing to hold onto. Traditional values, traditional beliefs, and traditional institutions are crumbling all around us. It seems as if the world is falling apart — and in many ways, it is.

It's precisely that experience of existential (what the maverick psychiatrist R.D. Laing calls "ontological") insecurity which makes it so hard to treat panic. The very institutions that are supposed to insulate us against a sense of spiritual emptiness — the family; science; organized religion — simply aren't quite as reliable as they once were. (The fastest-growing religions in America are the ones that say the world is about to come to an apocalyptic end.) Therapy itself is one of those institutions that is no longer able to do the stabilizing trick.

In this way postmodern panic resembles AIDS, which seems to me to be another uniquely postmodern disease. When someone gets sick with most any other kind of illness, his or her immune system is the doctor's chief ally. But with AIDS, it's the immune system itself that's under attack; the white blood cells that are supposed to do battle with disease are destroyed.

In the case of panic, it's necessary to go outside the now unreliable societal "immune system." Where is there to go? To the creative, historical, developmental process of building something new with the very stuff that's fallen apart. Because the one thing we can rely on in such unreliable times is that process; as long as there are human beings, there's history.

What's history got to do with it? you may object. *It's irrelevant, it's boring, and it's dead, dead, dead.* When most people think about history (if they think about it all), what comes to mind are ancient Rome; 1492 and Christopher Columbus; 1776 and George Washington; and other assorted dates, names and places from the unchanging "past."

What I mean by history, however, is the living, ever-changing process in which all human beings participate and which we all help to shape — whether we are conscious of doing so or not. Social therapy cures panic by helping people — including people who are experiencing the falling-apartness of our world to an extreme degree, people who are having "nervous breakdowns" or "psychotic episodes" — to resume their relationship with history. We don't help them to "understand" abstractly that "the cause of their problem is society." Rather, the social therapeutic approach to panic is to enable people to go (back) into history, to reconnect them to it. Imagine people looking at themselves in the societal mirror, which — because it is broken — distorts and fragments everything reflected in it. Social therapy helps them to see themselves — including the extremely disturbing and frightening experience of "breaking down" or "cracking up" that they're undergoing at this particular moment — in a total historical perspective.

When someone you're close to "loses it" in this way, you can use the social therapeutic approach to help them as well as yourself. No one has to panic in the face of panic; no one has to relate to it as if it were the end of the world. One very practical and immediate way to help is to listen actively to someone who's panic-stricken talk about the totality of his or her life. What else is happening that they care about, and how does it connect to history? A crisis, like a panic attack, is always just one of many, many things going on.

Ironically, it's only by being in history (going back to development) that people are able to "come back" to life in society.

But, you may say, *anxiety and panic seem a little technical and philosophical. What about good old-fashioned run-of-the-mill worrying?* Well, one nice thing about worrying is that it hasn't been taken over yet by the psychiatric establishment.

Let's take a look at Fran, who is 40 years old, a partner in a small, very successful public relations firm, and a self-described "worry wart." In fact, warts are among the many things she worries about. Fran also worries that she doesn't suffer from panic or anxiety, which she considers to have higher status than mere worrying.

One night she told her social therapy group what else is on her list, and how she does worrying: "I worry about what I'll do when I get too old to work. I'm afraid that I'll wind up on the streets, destitute. I worry that I'm not saving enough money, and that everyone but me is planning for the future or has something else going for them. I worry that the business could fall apart tomorrow and I couldn't get another job. I worry that in a few years the whole public relations field might become obsolete, and I'd be unprepared to do anything else."

In addition to her financial worries, Fran worries "more or less constantly" about her appearance ("I'm never going to lose weight — I'm becoming less and less attractive"), her sex life ("I'm going to be alone forever"), her health ("I could have cancer in me right now"), accidents ("I wonder what I'd do without my hands, or if I had to have a leg amputated"). She worries in every situation. When she has to make a presentation at work, Fran worries that she "may never have a good idea again." When she goes on vacation, she worries that she won't have a good time and she worries that she'll have such a good time she won't want to come back.

When she's with friends she worries that they don't really like her anymore.

Fran's philosophy, she said, is that "Life is a downhill slide — it gets harder and harder in every way. Everything is deteriorating and you have to be on your guard constantly." Fran even worries about worrying — she believes that "if you don't worry, you might get caught with your pants down."

Could any of the things Fran worries about actually happen? Yes. Of course, some are more likely to occur and some less; the chances that she is "poisoning" herself with every bite, for example, are pretty remote. Worrying, however, is an activity which often has little to do with what happens and a good deal to do with the age-old superstition that certain mental attitudes give people control over events.

In other words, worrying is primarily an illusory control mechanism. The illusion is that if you worry about something, you can somehow control it. But worrying that your mother may have cancer, that your teenage son is hanging out with the wrong crowd, that your husband is having an affair, that the promotion you were hoping for has fallen through, that you're eating too much, or that your insurance won't pay for your visits to the chiropractor, doesn't give you any more control over any of those situations than if, instead of worrying about them, you spent the same time at the movies or grooming the dog or taking a dance class.

Worrying is an impotent response to the experience of being impotent in a societal situation — the feeling that there's nothing you can do in that situation except to worry about it. As such, worrying (which people often do aloud) and obsessing (the "inner voice" of worry) tend to go back and forth, back and forth, back and forth from "problem" to "solution," from "identity" to "interpretation," without ever getting us anywhere.

Sexual impotence is one of those situations that men typically worry about. (Women do their share of worrying about men's impotence as well.) In social therapy, we say to men who are impotent, and to their partners: Don't worry about it! Don't try to solve the "problem." Don't get into thinking that you are what your penis is (or what his penis is). Don't try to interpret the impotence as "a sign" of anything. Instead, do the work to create an environment where you (given who you are) can give each other pleasure — an environment for the playful having of sex.

Often people who worry don't want to do that kind of work. They'd rather work when they feel like it and, when they're not "in the mood," they want to be able to retreat into their private universe where they can worry and obsess to their heart's content. They want to be comfortable.

Take Jack, who told the social therapy group that he's a worrier too, but "not like Fran." Jack tries to give the impression that he's the most responsible guy in the world because he's always worrying about everybody else. He worries about whether his 40-year-old daughter will be able to keep her job; he worries about whether his daughter-in-law, who's eight months pregnant, is eating right; he worries that his wife drives too fast; he worries that his partner is getting divorced; and he worries that his secretary's son goes to school in a rough neighborhood.

But while Jack's worrying appears to be much less self-centered than Fran's because he doesn't worry about himself, it's no less self-serving; he's still worrying for himself, just as she is. Like Fran, he always has to feel and to show that he's in control, despite the fact that he's not. He won't run the risk of being unguarded, of not looking good, of acknowledging that he doesn't know what to do. Jack may be worrying "about" other people, but in doing so he's trying to get something for himself.

While they may not look this way, worrying and obsessing are ways of avoiding life-work. As such, they're anti-developmental behavior. Worriers turn aside from the responsibility of creating their lives out of what there is. Instead, they preoccupy themselves with things as they are.

In the social therapy group, Fran asked what she should do to stop worrying. I suggested that she could give her worrying to us instead of using it to try to get something — control — for herself. The group, including Fran, decided to make her our "official obsessor": we would give her all our worries, and she would worry for (not about) us. More than that, she could come up with things to worry about that we hadn't even thought of.

This activity of "worrying for" is very different from worrying; it's a *conscious performance of giving* as opposed to the automatic getting behavior that "natural" worrying is. Fran went to work immediately at her new "job," and over the next several months it had a real impact on everyone. In the past, other people had been turned off by Fran's worrying. They experienced it as terribly self-centered, which it was. They would often use it as a justification for distancing themselves from her — which ("naturally") became yet another "problem" for Fran to worry about. Now, with Fran worrying for us, she was "a different person," as one member of the group said.

In fact, she was still Fran. But she was doing a different activity: she was genuinely giving (her concern, her intelligence, her imagination, her humor and her creativity) instead of getting. It allowed us to get to know her differently, to be more intimate with her, to give her more of ourselves — and for her to discover that she didn't have to be "alone forever" if she didn't want to be.

It wasn't hard for Fran to tell us her worries, because she thought (and from time to time still thinks) that it's necessary to worry. But she doesn't like to talk about her fantasies, she said, because then she'd be "giving away the possibility that they could come true… like telling a birthday wish."

This kind of fantasizing, which also gives the illusion of control, is a close relative of worrying; the "what" of it is different, but the activity is somewhat the same. It's not surprising that often people who do one of them a lot also do the other.

To fantasize or not to fantasize — that's not the question! From the social therapeutic point of view, there's nothing "wrong" with fantasizing. In fact, I think that creative, imaginative thinking is extremely positive when it's connected to work, to what we do with other human beings to create something new — and it can be very, very exciting. (Worrying, in my opinion, is simply a waste of this marvelously creative human faculty.) To the extent that it's disconnected from life, however, fantasizing (like worrying) makes us very vulnerable to the real world — vulnerable to feeling disappointed, hurt, isolated and impotent when reality doesn't conform to what we imagined.

The fantasizing that's next-of-kin to worrying rarely leads to creativity; it just "sits there" in our heads, or wherever, without going anywhere. But creativity — the producing of something new that comes out of our involvement in joint emotional, artistic and intellectual activities with other people, which is what social therapy means by development — often includes fantasizing of the richest, most exciting kind. When that's how you're living your life, you've got nothing to worry about.

EXERCISE:

This may help to give you a different perspective on worrying.

Worry for (not about!) someone else for a day.

20

Stress: The Fanatic Factor

Nancy, a very good friend of mine with a wonderful sense of humor, made a decision a few months ago to become a vegetarian. She had read several books about it, she told me, and concluded that eating meat was responsible for everything in her life that she didn't like: poor digestion, occasional grumpiness, the seven pounds she'd been wanting to lose for ten years. Once she made the decision, Nancy went (you should pardon the expression) cold turkey. It lasted a week. The next time I saw her, she told me that she had "fallen off the wagon" at brunch on Sunday. What happened? She ate a double helping of sausages. I couldn't resist teasing my ex-vegetarian friend a little. Grilled chicken I could see. Broiled fish, sure. But sausages? Nancy looked me proudly in the eye, and said: "I'm not a fanatic, Fred."

It's true. Nancy's one of those rare birds who isn't obsessively concerned, as so many people are in a culture of getting, with getting it right (whatever the "it" happens to be). And that's why she rarely has to deal with stress — at least as significant a factor in many diseases, in my opinion, as cholesterol.

Our culture of getting is, at the same time, a culture of meaning ("getting the meaning") and a culture of perfectionism ("getting it right"). Many people spend a good part of their lives trying to get "symbols" — things and other people — of worth. "Perfection" — like the activity of getting itself — is taken as a sign of how good we are as getters. This culture of getting/meaning/perfectionism is an environment that produces fanaticism. We are taught, in many ways, to admire fanatics — people who are obsessed with getting — as long as their obsession gets expressed in ways that are deemed societally acceptable. Yet that obsession is what produces one of the quintessential postmodern diseases: stress.

A great deal has been written about stress, the intense emotional and physical experience of pressure we have in situations that seem too big for us to handle. We feel uneasy, anxious, overwhelmed, unable to cope; we get headaches and stomachaches and backaches; we're nauseated, dizzy, sleepless and exhausted. Although some of us suffer more, and some less, almost everyone in our culture of getting is a victim of stress, and of fanaticism.

Fanaticism is the obsessive preoccupation with rightness and the equally obsessive fear of being wrong. As children, we are taught very early on never to say, "I'm wrong." When we are wrong, we're supposed to find ways of covering it up so we won't have to "admit" that we didn't get it right and thereby face being humiliated. Many of us become adults believing that the "point of life" is to avoid being mortified in this way.

For many people, it's particularly humiliating to risk not getting it right and to acknowledge being wrong in situations we're all supposed to be able to handle "naturally" — personal life. Hard as it may be to say that they were wrong about a decision they made at work, it's often much more difficult for parents to say that they were wrong about a decision they made concerning their children. Men are often more ashamed when they're unable to have an erection (which "means" getting sex "wrong") than they are when they can't meet a quota or a deadline.

I think being a fanatic is not conducive to mental health. Unfortunately, many people — including those who are (fanatically) anti-fanatic when it comes to politics or religion — are nevertheless practicing fanatics when it comes to the mundane activities of their everyday getting life. They're narrowly single-minded, convinced that they're right, bound and determined that everything has to be "just so." Living and working that way drives them and the people around them nuts. They're the ones, ironically, who are often most unwilling to learn something new; to do so, they'd have to admit that they haven't always gotten it right.

Take Ellen, who usually comes into her social therapy group on Wednesday nights a few minutes after it begins. Trying to enter the room as quietly as possible, she manages to drop something or trip over someone almost every time and then whispers an apology. A kind, abundantly energetic woman in her mid-forties, Ellen has been a dedicated union organizer for many years. She's always in a rush, wherever she may be — including the therapy group — so she often ends up going off in the wrong direction, forgetting something or someone she needed to take with her, elbowing other people out of the way, her mind "somewhere else" when someone asks her what she thinks. At the end of a day, she's "worn to a frazzle." She can't understand why she doesn't get more accomplished at her job, since she's "always working," or why other people are so often irritated with her. But when anyone tries to tell her, she's not very interested.

Larry, who's in the same group, appears to be Ellen's complete opposite. A 47-year-old architect, he's never held a job for more than a year; he either quits or is fired because he refuses to do things (like staying late to meet a deadline) that he regards as "unreasonable." Larry laughingly acknowledges that his definition of this word may be broader than most.

When a situation comes along that he doesn't like, Larry's liable to have a temper tantrum — or just not show up. Not surprisingly, the work atmosphere becomes increasingly unfriendly; sooner or later Larry and his employers part ways. There's a high turnover rate in Larry's personal life as well, friends and lovers being similarly unreceptive to his "hit-and-run" tactics. In the group, Larry goes back and forth between expecting everything and everyone to be perfect and going to pieces (sulking, complaining, blaming) when they aren't. Yet he's about as unwilling as Ellen is to learn what other people have to teach him about doing things differently.

This unhealthy combination of perfectionism and incompetence is a perfect set-up for stress in life and at work. Of course, work — like life — is filled with "imperfections." Computers crash, people blow up, accidents happen, mistakes are made. (You can add your own imperfections to the list.) But what's so bad about being wrong? The important question is: Now, what?

From a social therapeutic perspective, every moment — especially a "disaster" — is an opportunity to reorganize the total work environment. That isn't to say you'll succeed in reorganizing it. Maybe you can't, at that moment. But doing the work to transform totalities is an activity that produces mental health, because it's both energizing and relaxing; it helps you to be more competent. On the other hand, being obsessively fixated on getting this or that particular thing or person "fixed" so that "from now on things will be perfect," and stubbornly insisting that you know the answer and can impose it on the situation by the sheer force of your will, produces enormous stress — not to mention more mistakes, accidents and "disasters." Everyone else is compelled to keep one eye on the fanatics, who are always on the brink of falling off the ladder or otherwise going over the edge.

The social therapeutic approach helps people not to be ashamed of being imperfect, like my friend Nancy, and at the same time to be un-arrogant enough to want to learn how to handle life competently.

EXERCISE:

This will show you what it feels like not to be a fanatic.

Do something wrong just for the sake of saying: "I was completely wrong!"

21

Working Vacations

Molly, a member of one of my therapy groups, came back from a "dream" vacation that turned out to be a nightmare. The cast of characters included three of Molly's oldest friends, who live out of town, and Molly's closest friend at work, Helen, who had heard a lot about Deb, Renee and Felice but had never met them.

Felice wasn't enthusiastic about having Helen along, but Molly wanted her to come and Felice finally agreed. A few days before they were scheduled to leave, Renee called Molly to say that she and Deb had had "one of their arguments." (As Molly told her social therapy group afterward, Renee and Deb have been "fighting and making up since junior high.") Molly began having second thoughts about the vacation, which had been her idea in the first place.

They met at the airport in Los Angeles, and flew to Mexico City together. In the hubbub and excitement, they were all very gay and friendly to one another; Molly relaxed and decided that everything was going to be fine. When they arrived at the house they had rented for two weeks, everyone was thrilled. It was very beautiful, with a garden full of flowers — "perfect." They put their baggage down in the living room, changed into their bathing suits, and went outside for a dip in the swimming pool right away. That night, they had dinner in a restaurant and decided that when they got up each morning they would talk about what they wanted to do that day. They agreed that they didn't all have to do the same thing, but that they would plan their days together.

Then they came back to the house and "it all started to fall apart." Renee insisted on having one of the three bedrooms to herself because she's a light sleeper. Helen assumed that she would share a room with Molly, but so did Felice. Deb said she felt insulted because it seemed that no one wanted to be with her. While Molly's three old friends "carried on," Helen "just got quieter and quieter." When Molly tried to find out what was going on with her, Felice took the opportunity to tell Molly that she should "stop taking care of" Helen. Molly was furious with all of them for "acting like such babies and making me feel guilty, no matter what I did."

They finally worked out a compromise that seemed reasonable. (Renee got her own room, Molly and Helen shared one bedroom, and Deb and Felice shared the third; two nights each week Helen stayed with Deb and Felice stayed with Molly.) But it still "felt so awkward," Molly said — "especially because no one said anything."

Over the next two weeks, they continued not to talk to one another about how they were doing the vacation. They had some nice times, but there was "a lot of tension." Renee mostly wanted to sunbathe and eat in fancy restaurants, Deb wanted "to go everywhere and do everything," and Felice wanted to have heart to heart talks alone with Molly. As for Helen, "she kept saying that she shouldn't have come." Deb and Renee, who had made up by then, accused her of being "paranoid."

Back home, Molly has been talking in her social therapy group about her relationships with her friends, and the things she saw on the vacation that she hadn't seen before: Felice's possessiveness, Renee's self-centeredness, Deb's "touchiness," Helen's dependence. Molly also saw her own unwillingness to tell her friends what she wants and needs from them.

What Molly says reminds Gloria, another member of the therapy group, of the "vacation from hell" that she and a man named Patrick took a few months after they met. "I thought I was madly in love with him, but I found out that I hardly knew him." They stayed in the cabin in the mountains of western Massachusetts where Patrick had been going with his family since he was a little boy. The "idea" of the place is to "rough it" all the way — which came as something of a surprise to Gloria, whose idea of a good time is a luxury hotel. She had packed all her fanciest "resort" clothes, only to realize, after they got there, that anything except old flannel shirts and worn-out jeans was "weird." While Patrick went for an early swim every morning in the ice cold brook that ran through the property, she would sleep late, huddling under the blankets to stay warm. Gloria wanted to drive into "town" to shop, but Patrick explained that Main Street's major attractions were a store that sold snowmobiles, a 70-seat movie theatre and a large supermarket. He couldn't understand why she would want to go shopping, anyway, when there were trails to hike and mountains to climb. At night, when Gloria would have liked to go dancing or to the theatre, Patrick wanted to walk some more under the stars. "I felt like I was a fifth grader on a class trip to the planetarium," Gloria recalled. "He would try to teach me the names of the constellations, which I didn't particularly want to know."

One reason vacations sometimes don't work out is that the vacationers find themselves spending a whole lot of time with people they don't ordinarily see that much of in everyday life.

Friends, lovers and families typically spend just a few hours a day together at the most — and when they are in each other's company, it's likely to be in circumstances where they're doing something else besides spending time together. Then they get to the beach, the mountains or wherever, and suddenly they have all the time in the world to discover things that they never noticed in everyday life — things they may not especially like.

When vacations go sour, it sometimes has to do with who's having them together and how those people are living their lives with each other all year 'round. So here's a rule of thumb: If your life is going badly, the chances are that whatever you do to get away from it all (particularly if you're doing it with the people that your life is going badly with) will go the same way. It may be unfair, but that's how it often goes — unless you do some hard work!

The most pernicious myth of vacations is that you're not supposed to do any work when you're on them. But the truth is that it takes a lot of work, and a lot of energy, to organize a really good vacation. If you want to swim a lot on your vacation, then you need to make a plan that includes going where there's water, with people who won't insist that you spend every day sightseeing with them.

Oh, come on, you may be saying to yourself. *Isn't that painfully obvious?* Painful, yes. Obvious? Not necessarily. It's often the case that people who want to swim, or ride horses, or make love all day long on their vacations end up going to places where those things are impossible to do — or going away with people who can't or don't want to do those things with them. And they often ignore the fact that it's these very same friends and relations who don't do very much very willingly with them back home.

But the work of vacations doesn't just take place beforehand; it's necessary to build the vacation environment continuously, all the time you're "on vacation." You see, relaxation isn't just a matter of stopping what you usually do; it's doing a different activity. Just not doing what you're used to every day isn't, by itself, necessarily marvelous — even if you don't enjoy the daily routine. Ask any retiree with a lot of time on his, or her, hands and no plans. While two negatives may make a positive according to the rules of English grammar and of algebra, it doesn't always work that way in life. In fact, the assumption many people make that merely leaving a bad relationship, an unhappy marriage or a lousy job will make everything alright often leads to tremendous disappointment. (This, by the way, is why counseling or 12-step programs or diets, which concentrate on getting people to stop doing something that they've decided is negative, are often of limited value.)

This is not to deny that not doing certain things can sometimes yield considerable pleasure, or at least relief. It's just not the whole story. Once you've experienced the satisfaction of sleeping 'til noon on the first Monday of your vacation, you've got to figure out what you're going to do after that. If all you want to get from a vacation is the gratification that comes from not going to your job — then my advice is not to go anywhere. You'll also have the gratification of saving a bunch of money. Or you can do something positively different.

Now there's a certain kind of vacation you can take at home which can be a whole lot of fun, and very gratifying, because of what you are doing. What it requires, like every other kind of vacation, is shifting gears — changing pace, slowing down — mentally and physically. And you need to do this even if you're into doing a lot. Which is part of why you have to work on it.

In everyday life, much of what we do isn't gratifying in and of itself; it's a means to an end. We do it to get it done, to get it over with: giving the kids breakfast, depositing a check, catching the bus, writing a report, calling the plumber, doing the plumbing, having a meeting, making a sale, picking up the clothes from the dry cleaners, giving the kids their bath. Our everyday activities all tend to be overdetermined by considerations of time and money. They're functional. They're ways of getting something.

On vacations, however, we supposedly do things for the sake of doing them rather than for some other purpose. Walking on the beach, taking a ride in a horse-drawn carriage, sightseeing, shopping, getting your picture taken with Mickey Mouse, climbing a mountain or looking at the Mona Lisa are usually not means to an end, but ends in themselves. In other words, the point of vacations is to enjoy what you're doing. Which is why you want to slow the process down, and savor everything.

What you need to do is give yourself and others a break from the getting game. Vacations are a great time to practice giving; the best vacations are vacations from getting. A really gratifying, restful vacation, as I see it, is when people who care about each other get together and work to organize an environment in which they can just give to each other. *Sounds like too much work,* I can hear the cynic objecting. No. It's much more like play.

On vacations, as in life, what's most important is not what you're not doing but what you are doing. This includes, of course, how you're doing it.

A good vacation requires giving — including the conscious giving of energy to planning and organizing it. If you don't organize it — whether "it" is the rest of your life, a two-week vacation with your four best friends, a birthday party for your eight-year-old, or a romantic evening with the one you love — it isn't likely to be what you want.

Yes, satisfying and gratifying relaxation — breaking out of getting and into giving — takes a great deal of work. The good news is that working with people we care about to create an environment in which we can play together in new ways is much more than the necessary prerequisite for having a good time — it's what makes the good times so good.

EXERCISE:

Play the vacation game. (You don't have to have a vacation coming up to play.)

Get a vacation guidebook, sit down with someone you're close to, choose a place you'd like to go together, and talk about how you'd create an environment there in which you could be giving to each other all the time.

22

Shyness (and What To Say When You've Got Nothing To Say)

The social therapeutic approach is much more concerned with activity than with content. That people are talking to each other, making love to each other, and building something together is, from this perspective, of much greater importance than the what of it: what words they say, what sex they do, whether they build a bridge or a friendship. This is how I came to discover what to say when you have nothing to say. Whenever you feel that you have nothing to say, the thing to say is: "I have nothing to say."

Often, in therapy, people tell me they hate being at parties, or going on dates or visiting their relatives, because they have nothing to say in those situations. Or they try to explain why they aren't saying anything in the group by saying that they've got nothing to say. I always ask them to try saying just that. In 25 years of doing therapy, I have never met anyone who said "I have nothing to say" more than twice in succession, in any context, before finding that there was something else he or she wanted to and could say. In most cases, people only say it once and it elicits a response from the person they say it to which prompts them to say something different.

Let's say that you've just been introduced to someone at a party. You each say hello, and then there's a silence. You may think: "Here we go again. This is so awkward, so mortifying — one of those horrible moments when I've got nothing to say." But that isn't the case, because in fact there is at least one thing you have to say:

You: I have nothing to say.

Other Person: Me, too.

Now you've got something new to say. Or the Other Person might respond by saying: "Why not?" Or: "Do you mean that you have nothing to say to me, or that you have nothing to say, period?" And then you might have something to say to that. I'm not urging, by the way, that you say whatever's on your mind; honesty is not always the best policy, in my opinion. This is about saying something when nothing is on your mind! You rarely have to say that you have nothing to say twice, and once is usually enough, to produce the conditions for saying something else.

The point is that it's activity — in this case, the activity of talk-ing — which is fundamental. A friend of mine who lived for sev-eral years in a village in Nepal tells me that the people of Bhojpur were invariably pleased when she spoke their language, despite the fact that she wasn't at all capable of making sparkling conversation. As Connie describes it, her grammar and vocabulary made her "about as good a speaker as the average three-year-old," but she could say, very smoothly and politely, "I'm sorry. I don't under-stand." This always elicited kind smiles and approving nods. What mattered was that she was talking with them — not what they were talking about.

From the social therapeutic standpoint, people who think they have nothing to say tend to assume that the purpose of speaking is to talk about the world in such a way as to show that the speaker is "interesting," "witty," "perceptive," or "knowledgeable." In other words, they accept the societal convention that what we're doing when we speak to each other is producing language "tokens" that can be exchanged, in the "get and take" of ordinary conversation, for language of equal value. When speaking takes that contractual form, as it often does in the most heavily institutionalized situations — The Party, The Date, The Family Occasion — look at who's talking: societal Masks reciting lines from the appropriate scripts. When people say they have nothing to say, what they are likely to mean is that they feel unable or unwilling to participate in this competitive game.

But that's not all speaking is; it's also the activity of uttering words together with other people, where what matters is not what you're talking about but that you're engaging in the human activity of talking. There are many occasions when people do recognize the significance of speaking to be in the activity, and not in something outside of itself that it refers to: a baby's first words, a conversation between people who haven't been "on speaking terms," a poem, a lullaby, expressions of grief or tenderness or passion, all matter to us, regardless of what they're about.

In other words, aboutness ain't all it's cracked up to be. It's one dimension of conversation, certainly, and certainly it can be very useful for making statements and asking questions that refer directly to some other thing we want to know about or let other people know about: "How much does it cost?" "The house is on fire!" "Here are the keys." "Two eggs, sunny side up, rye toast and orange juice, please." "I have a sore throat." "When does the movie start, and where should I meet you?" But when it comes to emotions, aboutness is about as useful as a comb with no teeth. Often, the more you try to use it the worse things get.

Sometimes the initial response of people in a social therapy group to the statement "I have nothing to say" is to insist that it isn't "true": "Of course you have something to say! You're so intelligent, so accomplished..." But the social therapeutic approach is one of radical acceptance. We don't attempt to explain or interpret what people say, or to diagnose the "problem" that "caused" it.

Take shyness, which I think is probably an expression of many things, including a tendency to idealize what's supposed to be produced in a given situation (a display of extraordinary wit or brilliance or charm or skill or physical beauty). That tendency to idealize the world is typically accompanied by a sense of personal inadequacy, often acquired in childhood and left over from then, that makes us reluctant to go into the societal marketplace to compete for attention and approval with all the other contenders. The truth is that all you probably need to be "good enough" is to make comprehensible noises along with everyone else.

Shyness is also one of many manifestations of humiliation. A prevalent emotion in our culture, humiliation frequently manifests itself in extreme aggression, and all kinds of other self-degrading and abusive behavior. Many people in a culture of getting feel humiliated and ashamed; how could we not?

After all, we learn shame at a young age. Children are taught to cover up immediately: Put on your pants! Close the door! Do this! Don't do that! "Good" children are the ones who learn most quickly what to show off (how smart they are, how cute they are) and what to hide (mostly everything else). The message, which kids "get" very early, is that they have to hide who they are. Ours is a hiding culture.

Adults continue to feel very vulnerable to being exposed — to have others know that they're not really as smart, as competent, as together (as clean, or nice, or sweet-smelling) as they pretend to be; there's an element of pretension that often goes along with humiliation. People are afraid that, suddenly and without warning, their masks will be torn away and they'll be exposed to the world as an ordinary person just like everybody else. Humiliation is, in part, the product of our idealization of who we are, and our consequent vulnerability to having that idealized self-image stripped naked.

Sarah, a happily married high school teacher in her early fifties, came into her social therapy group one night and said she wanted to talk about something that had happened to her that morning. It was "nothing," she told us, "which is why I'm upset about letting it upset me." She had gone to get a haircut at a new place in her neighborhood, which appealed to her because it was convenient and probably less expensive than most. She walked in ("no appointment necessary") and got introduced to Gregory, the haircutter, who sat her down and said with a friendly smile: "You know what you need in addition to a haircut? I have a semi-permanent hair coloring to cover the gray..." Sarah smiled back, shook her head no, and said she just wanted a haircut. After a while, Gregory gave up trying to persuade her. In fact, he stopped talking altogether and cut her hair without another word. "Have a nice life," he said when she left.

Sarah was mortified. "I walked in there feeling fine, and I walked out feeling ugly and stupid," she told us. "He acted like there was something wrong with me for looking how I look, and — even worse — that I didn't know enough to know how bad I looked, or else I would have done something about it. I felt that he was laughing at me."

Now I wasn't there, but it's my very strong feeling that Gregory didn't care much, one way or the other, how Sarah looked. Incidentally, she looks exactly like who she is, a woman who's lived a rich and rewarding life which is getting better and better as she gets older. Gregory, I suggested to Sarah, was looking to make a sale, and he was perfectly willing to exploit her humiliation to do it. When it didn't work, he got nasty — and he let it show.

Then Sarah said she actually feels less humiliated now than she ever has before about how she looks. Frank, another member of the group, who's going on 60, said he knew what she meant. Having gotten older, Frank said, he's more comfortable with who he is and what he can do than he was as a younger man. Frank said he thought he was a more attractive 59-year-old than he was a 29-year-old. "I wasn't good at it — being attractive — and for all sorts of reasons I wasn't interested in it then," he told us. "I'm closer now to who I am. I don't feel I have to hide anything, and I think that makes me look better."

I agree. One way to deal with the humiliation that most of us feel about our physical selves is to know that it is likely to disappear as we get older and become less committed to hiding — and less able to do it.

Still, I think we all need to practice a radical acceptance of humiliation as a real part of who we are. What else could Sarah have done in the face of Gregory's attempt to turn her humiliation to his advantage? She could have said to herself: "Hmmm. He's successfully pulling my strings. I need to be aware that I'm still vulnerable to being manipulated in that way, when I thought that I had become immune to it." She could have let herself experience her humiliation instead of being humiliated by feeling humiliated and trying to hide that. It's in getting into feeling humiliated that you become less vulnerable to it.

Why? Because humiliation depends on hiding — just as depression depends on loss, and guilt depends on judgments. When we eliminate hiding, out goes humiliation. When we eliminate loss, out goes depression. When we eliminate judgments, out goes guilt.

The essence of the societal imposition of humiliation is contained in the finger pointing, jeering statement: "I can see your _____." The non-humiliated (or positively humiliated) response to that statement is: "Of course you can. I'm showing it to you."

Which is why, when you have nothing to say, the only thing to say is that you have nothing to say.

EXERCISE:

This is a way to take a look at humiliation.

Do something slightly embarrassing and don't try to cover it up; study it instead.

23

Do Talk to Strangers

Let's face it. If you want to meet new people, you've got to talk to strangers!

Where do you go to find them? Wherever: the next church social, the "personal" ads, the health club, your niece's wedding, the garage where you take your car for a tune-up, the company picnic, a conversational Italian class, your high school reunion, a business lunch... If you want to meet someone, then I think you have to avail yourself of all the different opportunities there are for doing that — and you have to be open to trying new ways. Go where you wouldn't dream of going — you might be surprised to discover that you're more comfortable in some "strange" places than you thought you'd be. You might be amazed to find that you enjoy being with people you thought you had nothing in common with!

One thing's for sure — you're unlikely to meet anyone where you've never met anyone before. If you've been going to the movies with your sister and brother-in-law every Friday night for the last eight months, do something new this Friday night. When you're looking to meet someone to go out with, don't hang around waiting for him or her.

Then what? People often end up being trapped in situations they don't want to be in because they're not good at creating the initial environment for getting to know each other — getting the conversation started. From a social therapeutic perspective, what's most important when it comes to meeting new people is not where you do it but how. How do you organize the activity of meeting? How do you create an environment in which you have the best chance of discerning whether the person you've just met is someone you want to know better — and whether you're someone the other person would like to know?

One way that I know of to organize such an activity, or environment, is to pretend you're a hitchhiker who's going the next 200 miles with "a perfect stranger" — someone you'll probably never see again. Talk about things you don't ordinarily talk about and be much more open and honest than usual. Use the fact that you don't know this person at all and might never see her or him again to "come out" as who you are, without being preoccupied with the question of whether anything will come of it.

At this very early point, neither of you has to have any investment whatsoever in making things work out — which makes meeting (or "first dating") a great opportunity to learn how to do something new. You can tell each other who you are without feeling constrained by the need to hide who you are so that you can "make a good impression." In my experience, "putting your best foot forward" virtually guarantees you'll trip.

In other words, don't try to set it up so that the other person will like you enough to want to see you again before you've even decided if that's something you want to do. Your attitude can be: "Let's make believe we've wound up in the same truck cab together — there are no promises to make, no expectations to meet, nothing between us. So let's talk until we get to the place where you're going to drop me off."

You say anonymity? I say creativity! I'm suggesting that you make positive use of the fact that you don't know each other, rather than turning it into a hurdle that you have to get over as quickly as possible so that you can go on to the "next step." The trouble with the activity of getting over is that it's entirely different from the activity of getting to know; if you're doing one, you almost certainly can't be doing the other.

"I just can't talk to complete strangers," people often say. But in fact, it's often much easier for us to talk with people we don't know well — or don't know at all. Why? Because we feel less humiliated in exposing who we are to people whose judgments don't matter all that much to us, and who are willing, if only for a few hours, to travel down the highway together and to share our shame. You see, it's *because* a first meeting or first date is limited — *because* it doesn't have to go any further — that you can be unusually intimate with a complete stranger.

Often people tell me that they feel too shy, or too embarrassed, or too inhibited, to expose who they are at first. But the fact is that most people are unlikely to get better at it. Many of us don't get less shy with people we "know better." We and they simply adapt to our shyness.

Take Rachel and Sonny, who have been dating each other for a year and a half. She's an elementary school music teacher in her early thirties, and he's a commercial artist a year younger. In a social therapy session I did with the two of them, Rachel said she feels humiliated because she "has to chase after" Sonny. He didn't know what she was talking about. Rachel explained that she often wished that Sonny treated her in the way that her brother-in-law treats his wife, Rachel's sister. Very reluctantly, Sonny said that he doesn't want to be "married." He's happy with their relationship as it is, and doesn't particularly want it to go "further." Rachel said that she felt she was "settling for second best" by dating Sonny "on his terms," and that she wonders whether she'll ever meet a man who will care for her in the way she dreams about.

Rachel and Sonny had no idea that they each wanted something very different from their relationship; they had never talked about it before. I've worked with couples who were married for 25 years and didn't know each other much better than this. They haven't become better at being intimate, just better at not being intimate.

So when you go out with someone for the first time, take advantage of the opportunity. Use what you've got. It's because there may not be a second time that this is someone you can be really open with! Here's how that first conversation over lunch or sitting on a park bench or taking a drive with the New Person might go:

You: I can't think of anything to say.

NP: Me neither.

You: Say anything.

NP: What high school did you graduate from?

You: I didn't. I got pregnant, and had to get married — at least I thought that's what I had to do.

NP: Oh — you have a child?

You: Yes, she's 10.

NP: What happened to your husband?

You: Well, at 17 I found myself married to someone I hardly knew and certainly didn't love. We split up. And for a long time I just sat around the house crying.

NP: That sounds terribly painful and lonely. How did you get over it?

You: You know, I'm not even sure. Sometimes I don't think I did get over it. But after a while I stopped crying and went out of the house.

Consciously organize your first meeting or first date (who knows if you want there to be a second?) as a very limited experience that doesn't have to "go anywhere." Then, put yourself fully into it. Remember, you can always change your mind. Of course, practice safe hitchhiking. But keep in mind that you're not a little kid anymore. It's okay to talk to strangers. If you're going to meet new people, you'll have to.

EXERCISE:

You know what to do!

Put yourself in a relatively safe situation, and find yourself a stranger to talk to. (If you don't have anything to say, take a look at Chapter 22.)

24

Decisions, Decisions, Decisions

Should you go back to school? Take that new job? End a love affair? Begin one? Bring your aging mother-in-law to live with you and your family? Move out of town? Undergo surgery? Have a child? How you do deciding has a lot to do with what decisions you end up making.

As a therapist, I often encounter people who hold dogmatically and fanatically to the assumption that it's critical to know what all the consequences are beforehand in order to make a decision. However, that's rarely possible. Nor, in my opinion, is it necessary. The decision to get a divorce or to change careers should, of course, be informed. But mainly such decisions set the stage for what will happen next; an infinite variety of unpredictable scenes can follow from them. Indeed, if that weren't true, why bother making the decision? All too often, people make major life decisions while hoping that somehow "everything will stay the same" afterwards. That's not a developmental way to live your life.

I don't even think that knowing what's going to happen in advance is what people usually use, or what they most need to have, to make important life decisions. Most of us tend to make both small and large decisions based on all kinds of things, including our beliefs, desires, attractions, preferences and values; our assessment (however unconscious) of whether this is something that will be in our best interests; what other people want and think (and what we think they want and think); and what we know, or think we know, about what our lives will be like if we say "yes" or "no." Or none of the above! In other words, we typically decide based on how things *look* to us, not on how they *are* — now *or* in the future. And many decisions are made intuitively. I don't think there's reason to believe that the intuitive ones turn out any worse than the others.

Again, this is not to say that getting all the information available on the subject isn't valuable. Is the new job likely to open up career possibilities for you? What do the people closest to you think about the relationship you're thinking of ending? How do they see the new person you've got your eye on? Does your mother-in-law want to live with you? Do you and your family want her there? What's the cost of living where you might be moving? What's the social life there like? The cultural life? The climate? The schools? What are the alternatives to surgery? What side effects and aftereffects can you expect? How do other people with this condition, of a similar age, tend to fare? The answers to questions like these can be useful in helping you to figure out what to do.

But while I am "pro-information," I think it's very important not to get locked into knowing what will, or has to, happen. Having such an idealized picture "in your head" tends to overdetermine how you respond when reality doesn't turn out, for better or for worse, as you thought it would. People are vulnerable to dropping everything, "going to pieces," or otherwise "losing it" when they're disappointed in this way. And when things turn out better than expected, being "locked in" makes it less likely that you will seize the unexpected opportunities.

From a social therapeutic perspective, there are two major conditions for making sound (developmental) life decisions. One is an active awareness of the fact that you don't, and can't, know how it's going to turn out and that this isn't a "problem." The other is to have no attachment to, or investment in, a preconceived, stereotyped, categorical notion of how it ought to turn out. You can't know what it's going to be like — but you can decide to do it anyway.

Take the decision to become a parent. If you don't have a preconceived, societally scripted play in mind (complete with a "happy ending") to which "the future" has to conform, you and your child can live and create a life together without getting bent out of shape someday — three hours, three months, three years, or 30 years down the road — because things aren't going the way they're "supposed to."

Again, try to know all you can. But don't get hung up on thinking that your knowing will make something turn out a certain way. It won't, and that's a good thing. If everything turned out to be just what we thought it would, there probably wouldn't be any such thing as development. Omniscience (another word for "wisdom") and development just don't go together.

It almost goes without saying — which is exactly why it's worth mentioning — that deciding to have or adopt a baby represents one of life's longer-term commitments. It's also likely to have a profound impact on the parents' financial, social and emotional life.

So in deciding to have or adopt a child you need to say something like: "I don't know how this is going to play itself out — I couldn't possibly — and that's okay. Without knowing in advance exactly what I'll be called on to do, or how I'll feel about it, I'm prepared to assume the responsibility of being a parent — whatever that turns out to involve. And that includes the likelihood that, at least some of the time, it will be difficult, expensive, painful and scary."

If this sounds like I'm talking about radical acceptance again, I am.

Under these conditions, you're *also* able to say, at any time at all in your child's life: "My goodness! Holy cow! Hell's bells! This job is a lot harder than I ever dreamed it would be. I thought it would be difficult — it's impossible! I thought it would be expensive — it's costing me an arm and a leg! I thought it would be painful — it's unbearable! I thought it would be scary — it's terrifying!" And that doesn't violate your commitment to your child. It doesn't "mean" that you're a "bad" parent, that you made the wrong decision, or anything else.

Of course, if you love every moment of it from the day your baby arrives on the scene, and everything is smooth sailing from then on — that's fine too. The point here is that many people can have a rough time of it and it's perfectly okay to say so. That's not being irresponsible; it's just having a rough time of it.

I think the way to decide whether you want to have a child or not — and in fact the way to make decisions, period — is to acquire the information that there is, explore what can be explored, and understand what you can understand, knowing that you don't know in advance how it will turn out. How could you? Why should you? Organize your life developmentally around the wonder that you don't.

EXERCISE:

You may find this helpful as a way to practice not knowing.

Make a decision based on much less information than you usually "need" and see how it turns out.

25

Don't Blame the Bully

Arlene describes herself as a "doormat" and says that "everyone takes advantage" of her — her mother, her teenage son, the other secretaries in her office. Even when she goes out with her friends on Saturday night, Arlene told her social therapy group, she never gets to say where she wants to go, or what movie she wants to see. "My friend Charlotte always gets her way. She bullies everyone else to go along with her. I wish I could be more self-assertive."

In a culture of getting, it's typical for groups of people, regardless of what kind of groups they are, to be organized in such a way as to produce "doormats" and "bullies" — societal roles that many of us first see acted out in the family, when we're still children. When getting is the name of the game, the competition is intense; in the rush to get more than their "fair share," the winners often end up stepping on the losers. Doormats and those who step on them — the bullies — are made in such environments, where no one is willing to call "Time out!"

Jim, for example, is a 34-year-old high school chemistry teacher who was regularly beaten up by his brother (Johnny was three years older) from the time that Jim was seven or eight until Johnny left home ten years later. Why did Johnny hit him, or threaten to? "It was usually because he wanted something that I had," Jim told the social therapy group the night that Arlene introduced the subject of bullying. "He'd try to take something away from me, and when I wouldn't give it to him he'd hit me. I would fight back, but he was bigger and taller than I was. I could never win. After a while I just gave in. When we got a little older, we sometimes used to play cards for money — if I was winning he'd start a fight. There'd be a commotion, and then my mother would come in and say, 'Okay, boys. That does it. No one wins. Both of you go to your rooms.'"

Jim hardly ever told his parents that Johnny hit him. "They both worked, so they usually weren't around to see what was going on. The few times I tried to say anything, I could tell that they didn't really want to hear it. My father couldn't stand arguments, let alone fighting — he was the big peacemaker in the family. As for my mother, she was always telling us that except for her and Dad, Johnny and I only had each other so we had to get along. But mostly I didn't talk about it because I was scared of what my brother would do to me. I just tried to keep out of his way. I used to daydream a lot about someday getting even with him. I certainly don't want my son to grow up to be a bully, but I also don't want him to be a pushover — what Arlene calls a 'doormat.'"

The social therapeutic approach is group-oriented. Increasingly, we are working with very large groups, which may have 100 or more people in them. We find groups especially helpful in showing group dynamics in a culture of getting — the role- and rule-governed behavior characteristic of groups (whether a family, a crowd of friends, a classroom, an office staff, a bunch of volunteers, a busload of tourists traveling together), which are organized as environments where individuals compete with one another to get things for themselves. Some people are more successful at this behavior, and others are less so, but that's what everyone is doing because that's often what the typical group environment supports them to do.

Individuals characteristically come into social therapy wanting the group to help them solve their "problems," including the "problem" that they're not "self-assertive" enough — which is often just another way of saying that they want to become better bullies. They compete with other members of the group to "get on the air," they "identify" with what other people say as a pretext for talking about themselves, and they give as little as possible.

The "assigned" task of the social therapy group is to work consciously to create an environment where giving, rather than getting, is the primary activity. Unless we organize it otherwise, any group in our getting culture will quickly become a place where "bullies," "doormats," and those who acquiesce to both, flourish. By participating in building an environment where the principal activity is giving, the members of the group discover, among other things, that there are no "individuated problems." They learn how to make creating such giving environments a life activity — that is, to practice it continuously — and, in doing so, they reinitiate their emotional development.

What grows and develops in social therapy, and in a life healthfully lived, is the group, not the individual. We challenge, in practice, the commodified, individuated notion of continuous individuated growth. Group growth, the growing environment — not an environment where individuated individuals grow — produces individual-in-the-group development. By giving to the group you grow as a member-of-the-group. In such environments, the growth of the group and the growth of its members are qualitatively inseparable.

As a result of the work that we have been doing in the social therapy group, Jim and his wife have begun to make their family a giving environment in which their young son can see that no one has to choose between being a "bully" and being a "doormat."

The social therapeutic approach doesn't help people to become more "self-assertive" but to become more creative. We understand the individuated "self" — individuated "identity" — to be a "self"-serving fiction. From my point of view, traditional psychology's obsession with measuring this fiction's esteem for and awareness of "itself," and with labeling and treating people for not having enough "self-esteem," contribute substantially to the misery-madness quotient in our getting culture.

In the social therapy group, I asked Arlene if she was asking for help to become more like Charlotte, who always gets her way. Does she want to become a successful bully also? Then everyone else will have two of them to go along with. If all you want is to get your own way, you can always just go off on your own and save everyone — including your "self" — the trouble.

Or, I asked, was Arlene saying that she wanted to be in a different *kind* of environment, where people decide what they want to do together rather than self-ishly. Did she want to learn how to be at ease as a giver in a culture of getting? If so, then she had to take a look at the totality of the Saturday night environment — how it's organized — and not just blame Charlotte, the bully. After all, as Arlene herself says, everyone else goes along with her.

Arlene says she feels like a "doormat" in all kinds of situations. Like a lot of other people, how she's living her "group" life doesn't produce any sense that she's part of something that's growing, or changing, or developing. She isn't. From a social therapeutic standpoint, Arlene has to change the totality of her life — she has to help create a bunch of giving and growing life environments.

Can she do it? Yes! In my opinion, it's actually easier for a "doormat" to transform his or her entire life than to beat up on the bully — especially in an environment that encourages bullying.

EXERCISE:

Here's how you can practice an "environmentalist" approach to bullying.

The next time you find yourself in a group with a bully, say to everyone: "It's our fault that he [or she] is behaving that way" and take it from there.

26

Matters of
Life and Death

Recently someone in a social therapy group was talking about her mother, who had had a stroke; since then, she said, her mother has "lost her personality." As a therapist, I hear about loss all the time: one patient is anxious that she'll lose her husband to another woman, another is afraid that he'll lose his temper on his job. And people grieve over what they feel they have lost: one patient is mourning her father, who died of cancer a few months ago, another says she has lost her looks. Loss, most "sane" people would agree, is a central reality of our getting culture. You can get it, and you can lose it. That's a basic rule of the societal game.

From the social therapeutic standpoint, however, the concept of loss is a societal illusion — an extremely powerful and compelling myth in our culture of getting, to be sure, but an illusion nevertheless. Before you "lose" this book in the trash can, or think that I've "lost" my mind, let me say more.

In our society, the very painful experience of loss, and the understandable fear of it, are extremely common. But I believe that there's no such thing as loss in history. Similarly, optical illusions are commonplace in ordinary perceptual experience by virtue of how ordinary perception is organized. Yet some physicists will tell you that there's no such thing as an optical illusion in subatomic reality because subatomic reality (which is at least as real as the "life-size" objects of everyday life) is perceived in a qualitatively different way. There can be mistakes, but not optical illusions. So it is, in my opinion, with loss and history.

History is the ever-changing totality of human life activity — the multidimensional, seamless, beginning-less, middle-less and end-less activity of life that we as human beings continuously and collectively create. There's no loss "in" history because there's no dimension outside or "beyond" it where "lost" things could possibly have gone. Contrary to what we're taught in our societally overdetermined culture, there's no time (no place called "the past") and no location ("heaven," "hell," or "the subconscious") in history where "lost" loves and "lost" opportunities and "lost" causes end up. Nothing completely new comes into existence in history and nothing goes completely out of existence.

Society, however, is quite a different kettle of fish. Society is a very particular, somewhat arbitrary arrangement of a unique "segment" of history. It is defined in terms of categories (such as the Western notions of "time" and "space") which are used for many purposes, including the preservation of society itself. In many societies, including our own, the rule-governed behavior associated with roles, not creativity, is dominant. In our postindustrial society, we are also typically alienated — removed from — the social process of production (including the "production" of our emotions). We see ourselves only as individuated selves with a fundamentally passive relationship to the world, and not as members of a species which collectively and actively produces everything that's made. So we believe that this arbitrary arrangement called society is all there is — or can be.

Which brings us back to history (not that we can ever really leave). As I have written about extensively elsewhere (for example, in my book *The Myth of Psychology*), I believe that the epidemic of depression in our culture is directly connected to our societally induced "amnesia" regarding history. Given our consequent vulnerability to loss, it's normal to be depressed. The social therapeutic approach treats depression by getting rid of (deconstructing) the societal illusion of loss — just as we treat humiliation by getting rid of (deconstructing) the societal illusion of "my-ness." We teach people to build environments that allow them to know themselves and one another in history — where they have nothing to be ashamed of, and nothing to lose.

That isn't to say, of course, that there isn't change, or that there isn't transformation. Certainly there are biochemical changes and societal changes; there's transformation (the developmental, the not-so-developmental and the nondevelopmental kind).

But loss? Not in history.

Are the particular chemicals or chemical arrangements that used to be part of us lost? Or does something have to be of a certain size in order for us to identify its no-longer-thereness as a loss — and if so, precisely what size? How big does a personality change have to be before we can appropriately say that someone's "lost her personality"?

Have you lost the time it's taken you to read this book? Have I lost the time it's taken me to write it? Do you lose your youth? Your family? Your life? Do you lose interest in someone you used to like? When does loss begin — a second after we've done or said something? A week? A year?

What about death? In a social therapy group a patient named Kathy said: "I worry about dying...I have a very difficult time when I think that this is all there is. I want there to be something else, something more — I want there to be a meaning to life beyond itself."

Was Kathy implying that if she were immortal, life would somehow be "justified" — would have a "point"?

Then someone else in the group, Tina, talked about trying to live her life in such a way that she would be remembered. I said she seemed to be taking the position that, if she were immortal (and therefore never "remembered" because she would never have left), then there would be absolutely no point to life! Why? Because if you believe that the point of life — given that we're *not* immortal — is to do what you have to do to *become* immortal, it follows that if you were immortal life would have no point.

What "point" was I trying to make? I was playing a language game with Kathy, Tina and the rest of the group, challenging them to take a look at the assumptions they were making by lumping together death and immortality and life-having-a-meaning (a "point"). In response to someone's question, I said I didn't know if their assumptions were "religious" or not, but if they were saying that they wanted to be "remembered," then that requires death — including the creation of monuments, emotional and otherwise — to replace what's been "lost."

What's so important about being remembered? Well, I think it's important in our culture because it creates the illusion that we still exist, whether we're dead or merely away on a trip. The need for this illusion is based, I think, on yet another — and perhaps the ultimate — self-centered illusion: the only thing that really exists is "me" and "my" experience. *Oh, come on!* you may want to say to me. *Aren't you exaggerating? Most people don't go around thinking that there's no one else in the world except for them.* Actually, I think that illusion is quite "natural" in our culture. Just think of most people's tendency to take what other people say and do "personally."

Social therapy helps people come to terms with the historical fact that there is an infinitude of activity, "past" and "present," out there which has nothing to do with whether we perceive it or not. It's in coming to terms with that fact that we are freed up to live in history — which is to live without loss.

What we create in life — a family, a business, a poem, a reputation, "good works" — is what we create in life. It will go on in all kinds of complex ways after we're dead. What the social therapeutic approach questions is why we should be motivated in life by what might or might not get done with what we create after we're gone. Why do we have to "leave a legacy" in order for our lives to have "meaning"? Why shouldn't we do what we do in life, for life, as a part of life, without bringing death into it at all? Why do we need to have a "reason" or a "motive" for living? Why do we need to "feel" that we're alive, to "know" that we're alive, or to "prove" it? After all, we are alive! As I see it, that's a fundamental fact of historical life. Why isn't that good enough?

"I'm afraid of death," Ben tells his social therapy group. "It's a void. A nothing. Nothing happens after you die."

Of course, Ben doesn't mean this literally. Or does he? Nothing happens after you die? Did nothing happen before you were born? We're no more or less gone, as far as anyone can tell, after we die than we were before we were born. What's the distinction between before-I-was-born and after-I-die? It can't be consciousness, since (again, as far as anyone knows) we're not aware before we're born that we don't exist. And we're characteristically not saddened by that fact.

Ben objects: "I don't miss what happened before I was born. But I feel like I will miss being here when I'm gone. It's not the same! Now, while I'm here, I feel sad when I think that someday I won't be."

That makes sense to me. But how is that the difference between not having been here before we were born and not being here after we're dead? How can how we are now be the difference between how we were before and how we'll be after? Only if you take life (your life) to be the dividing point between before and after. In society there are birth certificates and death certificates.

But not in history. If our emotional lives are overdetermined by who we are in civic society, they will be quite different from an emotionality based on our historical lives.

From the social therapeutic perspective, this kind of thinking isn't obscure philosophical nitpicking. Rather, we view these questions — and, more importantly, the activity of asking them — as tools (language games) designed to deconstruct the philosophical and linguistic patterns that both organize and justify our societal alienation.

The prospect of giving up subjective alienation — our culturally induced habit and privilege of standing back from life and looking at it as an "impartial" observer, a stranger to whom it must be "justified" — in favor of simply living life with the utmost intensity (as very young children do) can be quite frightening.

What's so scary about it? Many people think that if they wholeheartedly threw themselves into this activity of living, their lives might go by "just like that" — over before they knew it. Now that could be the experience...it's possible. I don't think, however, that it has to be. In fact, the very notion that life is something to be "experienced" is a big chunk of the very cultural structure we're trying to break down. You might experience your life going by in a moment — unless you gave up the ability, or the "prerogative," to make judgments as to whether or not life is momentary, worth living, or anything else. There's no evidence that a baby drinking its milk ever thinks: "Mmmm. Not bad. This is one of the best bottles I've had lately. Not as good as breakfast the day before yesterday, but definitely one of the top ten this week. I'd give it an A-minus." Nor is there any evidence that babies are missing anything by not making these kinds of judgments about life as they live it.

Joan tells the group that she used to say to herself all the time: "Watch out! Wake up. You're going to die before you know it."

Now she only does that once in a while. She says she doesn't know how "to finally break out of that trap."

I ask her why it has to be "finally."

Joan gives me her best *aren't-you-ever-satisfied?* look. "Because if it's not final," she says, "it doesn't seem real." It doesn't really count, if she's still "counting on" death to justify her life, even if it's only once in a while.

"Okay — just stop doing it altogether," I suggest to her. Is that different from "finally"? Joan wants there to be a moment when she'll have this down for sure. But there isn't such a moment: "for sure" is not where it's at in the disorderly environment of history.

That makes people anxious. We want something to be for sure: time, space, a higher authority, our selves (identity). But what if nothing is? What if nothing is final? Or for sure? What if what we have is simply what we have?

Sondra says that the "finally" is what motivates her; if there's no end point, when you've "got it" at last, then "everything's too hard." She'd prefer to do nothing — just watch television and sleep. She's asking for some kind of guarantee that she won't "slip back" — that she can eventually stop working at this. "Otherwise, forget it. Why keep doing it over and over again?" Sondra wants to know what the point is of there being no point. She insists that it's only if there's "a point to it all" that it's possible to do anything.

I ask her how she knows this. What I know from the years of work we've done together is that in fact it's pointlessness that has most helped Sondra to do new and developmental activities. When her life has been organized around "points" she's tended to be depressed, paralyzed, unable to do very much.

Whenever someone asks me why they should do this or that if life is pointless, my response is: That's precisely why you should do it — because it's not such a big deal as our culture of getting (the point) insists.

EXERCISE:

This may help you get the pointlessness of it all.

Do three completely pointless things today — and work very hard not to connect them with the rest of your day, even if they turn out to be wonderful.

27

Such Language!

Some of you may wonder where I'm coming from, theoretically. This chapter and the next are for you. I've put them last because, in my opinion, that's where theory belongs — not only in books, but in life. Children learn to speak, for example, long before they know the rules of grammar, or even that there is such a thing as grammar. Fortunately, it's unnecessary to be knowledgeable in anatomy and physiology in order to breathe, to master physics in order to throw a ball, or to study biochemistry to be able to eat a pizza. As far as anyone knows, biochemists don't "get more" out of "a slice with everything" than other people do.

I'm not making an argument for "know-nothingism" here; I simply want to keep theory in its place. Read these chapters at your own risk! Or don't read them at all — it's not required, and you won't get less credit if you skip them.

The underlying assumption of most ordinary conversations between people who speak the same language is that we understand what the other person is saying. And if we don't, we can always ask. Central to this assumption, in our culture, is a representationalist model of the relationship between language and the world, or "reality." In other words, we assume that our words are about something — they refer to, or represent, or mean, or denote, what exists objectively, "out there." This is the case even if the "out there" happens to be "inside" of us, like a gall bladder, a tooth, a desire, a pain, or an intention.

Regardless of what a particular conversation may be about, we typically take its about-ness for granted. As participants in a conversation, our job is to find out what the other person is talking about so that we can know what he or she is saying about that aspect of the world which is represented by his or her words. Not everything we say has this characteristic, but the model (the paradigm) of language is representational. "What's that person talking about?" and "What's that person saying?" mean roughly the same thing in our culture.

This way of understanding language, which comes "naturally" to us, apparently goes all the way back (like so much else, good and not so good) to ancient Greek civilization. As modern science and technology evolved in western Europe during the 18th century, the representationalist model became even more deep-rooted; their attempts to describe and control the natural world have been highly effective. "Objective" scientific language as the "representative" of nature has turned out to be quite useful.

But over the last hundred years or so, it has become plain to many people that, used in this way, language is totally inadequate for a human science concerned with understanding human life better. Psychology modeled on physics has been less than successful.

It was hard enough for the natural sciences to find language capable of comprehending the stars, atoms, quanta or dinosaurs. They did it largely through mathematical "translations" and advances in the technology of empirical observation. But if "hard science" language occasionally obscures more than it reveals, clinical psychological language which purports to be "about" emotions is often so vague as to be almost completely incomprehensible. What in the world is represented by words like "motive," "desire," "anger" and "panic?"

Speaking social therapeutically, there's not much basis for the presupposition that people actually know what they're talking about when they talk to each other about their emotions and other so-called "mental states." Yet people in our culture, influenced by the representationalist model, presume that they do. In my opinion, many, many difficulties follow from this.

Take words like "core," as used in phrases like "the core of my being" and "my core beliefs." Or "identity," as used by the late psychoanalyst Erik Erikson. Or that all-important thing called "self." Every one of them implies that they represent something, and they're all understood as such.

In an ordinary conversation, when one person says: "I feel shaken to the core," the other person is unlikely to subject such language to scrutiny: "What do you mean, core? Where is your core? When did you get it? How do you know you have one? Apples can be eaten to their cores, but can people be shaken to them?"

Or when one person says: "I'm having an identity crisis," the other person is not apt to say: "What do you mean, identity? You have one, and it's in danger? Does everyone have one? Is everyone supposed to have one?"

Such questions would be regarded as childish or foolish; both the speaker and the person spoken to in our psychologized culture assume that they understand each other.

Or take the word "past." It's not specifically a psychological term, but it's often used in a psychological context. The "past" is always spoken of as if it were a place in "time" that no one can go back to. But the "past," it seems to me, isn't a place at all — it only sounds that way. Like "core" and "identity" and "self," it is full of representationalist bias. So is the "future," which is also always spoken of as if it were a place. The difference is that at least some of us are expected to get to it "in time." But the future, in my opinion, isn't a place any more than the past is. The future — if there is one — is the continuous reshaping of the past; it's best seen as an activity rather than as an object. Our linguistic biases, however, make it very hard to see it that way.

It was feminists who first argued that there's a built-in male bias to the representationalist model of language. The model says: Here's the world, there's the sentence. Let's get them together. Over many, many millennia, it's mostly been men who have gone out into the world to discover what "the sentences" stood for. That cultural-historical experience has tended to make men worldlier and smarter — according to the prevailing male standards — than women, who as women have a very different cultural experience. It is out of their characteristically masculine experience of the world that men are usually more "forward-looking" than women, who don't so easily go into "the great unknown" because historically they haven't been allowed to do so. We don't hear too much about the great women explorers, in part because there haven't been a whole lot of them.

Women tend to understand and to be more at home with the past — what there is — but not how to represent or transform it. Men are better at the activity of transformation — creating the future — but they don't know the materials (the past) as well as women do. How could they? Historically, it's women who have been much more closely involved in the cyclical processes that are closely connected to the immediate biological needs of other people. While women typically think in more human terms, men tend to think in "god-like" ways; they assume that they're capable of creating something out of nothing. None of this is genetically determined, of course; it has to do with the different kinds of activities in which men and women have been engaged for most of the last million years.

For these and hundreds of other gender-based cultural reasons, men and women relate to language differently. If representationalism is "male-identified," women tend to have a clearer sense of language as creative, social activity — because, among other things, they're mainly the ones who play language games with young children.

Nowadays, whole books are being written about the fact that men and women who seem to speak the same language actually don't. I think that's true. Moreover, I am saying that men and women mean something different by, and do something different with, language itself. Both men and women find that frustrating and hard to understand. Often we share the same house. We may be bringing up children together. And yet it is remarkably common for men and women (even those who live together) to feel that they don't know what the other is talking about despite the societal assumption that they do. They often don't. Many of the fights that take place between men and women are actually fights over language — not just the meaning of this word or that word, but how they do language.

Al and Diane are a married couple in their early thirties. In a social therapy session, Diane says she wishes Al would tell her "once in a while" that he loves her deeply. Al says he doesn't understand why she wants him to say those words. Speaking as a representationalist, a man, Al's position is that Diane already knows the information represented and described by the words "I love you deeply." It seems to him, he explains, that it would be like telling someone that two plus two is four, or that George Washington was the first president. From his point of view, this "love talk" is silly, a waste of time.

Diane sees it very differently. She's not asking for information; she wants Al to participate in an activity with her that, for lack of better words, I'll call love/language-making. It isn't about anything (which is precisely what bothers Al); it is what it is in the same way that the playing of young children is what it is. It's the activity, not the meaning or reference, that matters.

Our clinical colleagues the "communicationalists" — therapists in the tradition of Gregory Bateson, Paul Watzlawick and others who have made invaluable contributions over the last several decades — help people to get along with each other better by working to clear up the linguistic confusions we all unavoidably get into. The communicationalists believe, as social therapists also do, in the need to challenge the presumption — which is especially strong in families — that people know what they mean when they talk to each other. The communicationalists teach people to talk about what they're talking about. They've come up with a technique, "meta-dialogue," that's designed to get rid of the confusion created at the "object level" — the level of ordinary conversation, where words are supposed to represent "objects" in the world. On the meta-level, the communicationalists say, it's the communication itself which counts.

Here's an example of what the communicationalists do.

Members of a family, who can't stop fighting, come into therapy. Fourteen-year-old Patti is furious at her father: "You're always telling me what to do. I can't stand it. I can't stand you. Leave me alone. I wish I were dead."

Dad is equally furious: "I'm always telling you what to do because you don't know what to do. You use bad judgment. Someone has to have some sense around here."

Mom sides with Dad: "I don't know what's gotten into you, Patti. We just can't talk to you anymore. Your father only wants what's best for you."

The communicationalist tries to get the three of them to talk about what they're doing when they speak these words — to have a meta-dialogue that gets beyond the original conversation. If the communicationalist is successful, Patti, Dad and Mom connect in a way they couldn't when they were talking at the object level.

In a meta-dialogue about that conversation, Patti might say: "What I'm doing when I say those words is expressing my desire to live my own life and make my own mistakes. I don't want you to interfere — even if you're right and I'm wrong."

Dad might say: "What I'm doing when I say those words is trying to show that I'm doing my job as a father — which means that I have to have all the answers."

And Mom might say: "What I'm doing when I say those words is showing my appreciation for the fact that your father is taking responsibility for what happens to you, and not leaving me to deal with it on my own."

As this hypothetical meta-dialogue reveals, the assumption that Patti and her parents were doing the same thing at the object level turns out to be false. In fact, no one knew exactly what anyone else was talking about. By focusing on the communication itself, the meta-level dialogue makes it possible for all of them to see that at the object level they weren't talking about the same thing and disagreeing. Rather, they were each doing something different. At the meta-level, they are doing the same thing. They're using language to show how they're using language. All three of them are saying: "When I say this, I'm doing that..."

The point is not that Patti and her parents agree now, but that going to the meta-level allows them to "bypass" their confused and contradictory disagreements on the object level so that they can "agree," in practice, to talk about their talking and their uses of language.

It's often the case that misunderstandings are at the root of family disagreements and breakdowns. Sometimes those misunderstandings last for months and even years, with husbands and wives, parents and children, fighting on and on without ever quite knowing what their loved ones — who are also their adversaries — are saying. Yet everyone assumes that they know exactly where everyone else is coming from.

As I understand it, communicationalists think that meta-dialogue is helpful to people because it allows them to break out of language-influenced contradictions and emotional "double binds" to clarify what they're talking about. In other words, meta-dialogue helps people to do "about-ness" much better than they did it on the object level.

From the social therapeutic vantage point, meta-dialogue can be helpful to people because *consciously* performing language as an activity helps to minimize the representationalist bias of language. In conducting a meta-dialogue, the family members are no longer under the impression or making the assumption that the words they're saying stand for something in the world — and that what they are saying about it is right. By talking about how they talk, they're talking to each other in a different way. They're engaged in a conscious performance rather than "natural" discourse. In playing this language game, they're actively creating something new together.

Donna has been living with Mike for six months; they're engaged to be married. When his parents called to say they were coming to town, she asked her social therapy group for help in doing "The Meeting." Donna thought it was highly unlikely that her future in-laws would like her; they have told Mike that they blame her for his decision to leave law school and become an elementary school teacher. "I don't know how to deal with their nastiness," she told us. "Mike's father acts like he's broken the law, instead of just choosing another profession — and I'm his accomplice."

In other words, Mike's parents are laying claim to their son, and they view Donna as the competition. How can she deal with it? By refusing to participate in the private property contest. Then she won't be vulnerable to their "nastiness" — or any other competitive tactics. They have to deal with their desire to own their son — she doesn't.

How should Donna not participate? Now's the time when the meta-language technique can come in handy.

Here's how it might go. Mike and Donna and his parents sit down to dinner. Before they've gotten to the main course, Mike's father is telling them that he thinks Mike is ruining his life. And Mike's mother is asking Donna if she's thought about what kind of life they're going to be able to have on a teacher's salary.

Rather than storming out, or blowing up, Donna could not participate in this conversation by talking instead about how they are talking.

She could ask the meta-linguistic question: "Why are we talking to each other like this?" She could make the meta-linguistic statement: "I think that this way of talking is hurtful to everyone." And she could insist — in a non-hostile way — that they respond meta-linguistically.

In the course of their meta-linguistic dialogue — their talking about how they are talking — the four of them could decide to declare a truce for the duration of the meal and, hopefully, of the visit.

Can Donna change the whole situation so that Mike's parents will be overjoyed with their son and with the life choices he's made? Maybe not. But she could do something that's in-between changing everything and taking part in some nasty behavior. By initiating a meta-linguistic dialogue, Donna would be doing something assertive to create an environment that would thereby be at least partially changed — one that was no longer overtly hostile or abusive. In this way, these four people whose lives are connected might begin to do something different with one another. Maybe they could talk about their favorite movies, or listen to some music — an experience which would enhance the possibility that they could continue to do something new.

Yet while I think that meta-dialogue can be a useful technique for helping people to do something different in such situations, the social therapeutic approach doesn't teach people to go beyond the object level of language to a meta-level of discourse. Why? Because I believe that this "solution" merely avoids the overdetermining representationalist bias of ordinary communication. It's a fancy "trick" (what philosophers sometimes call "a type theoretic solution") to get people to talk to one another without actually addressing the systematic contradictoriness that's embedded in the presuppositions of "real-life" dialogue.

Yes, you may get clarity in the meta-dialogue. But it might be a false clarity. And yes, it is something new. But it might not be developmental. It still relates to language as fundamentally pure representationalist communication, with a rule to get you out of the binds. It's still stuck in about-ness; the meta-dialogue is about the object-level dialogue.

My point is not that the communicationalist approach is flawed "in theory." By going beyond the object level to the meta-level, the communicationalists don't go far enough in practice.

Their position is that communication is all there really is. The communicationalists' concern is not to change behavior, or to discover meanings, but to enhance the quality of communication. Now that's certainly a valuable thing to do. It can be very useful, in the way that cleaning a word processor is. But it runs the risk of reinforcing the assumption that language, and in particular emotive language, merely conveys information.

The implicit assumption that what we say necessarily refers to something outside itself derives directly from the representationalist model of language. Now we all know, of course, that not every word denotes something. Not every sentence is about something. Language doesn't only represent. Yet there is a more important point here. While in our culture we may all tend to think of language as a "thing" that represents other things, I believe that language is best viewed and practiced as a creative collective activity that human beings engage in.

The social therapeutic approach views language not only as a ready-made societal tool which we as human beings use in the representationalistic form in which we found it "when we got here." For it is critical to recognize that we, as individuals and as a species, are language makers — creators — as well as language users. Very young children create language anew, often in conjoint activity with adults, not merely for a particular use ("I want my bottle!") but for creativity's sake, just as poets do: for the sake of the very human activity of creating community together — in this case a language and cultural community in which we can, among other things, create and build still more.

In my view, emotional discourse is far more like making poetry together than it is like "scientifically" describing "reality." The social therapeutic concern, therefore, is not simply to help people clarify information, but to make meaning together. We regard the making of meaning as a critical dimension of language — in particular, of emotive language. The trouble with meta-dialogue, from the social therapeutic point of view, is that it leaves out language as shared, creative activity.

In social therapy we work to teach this creative and activistic understanding of language in the process of helping people to do their emotions differently. For language, especially emotive language, is not merely to be used. It's to be created and creative with. It's not merely functional — it's poetic.

What Mom, Dad and Patti are saying — as they make clear in their meta-dialogue — is that their words represent "reality" positions; their use of words is purely "functional." The function? To defend their positions. In talking this way — that is, in using words to represent and defend "reality" positions — they're allowing themselves to be led around by their representationalist and functionalist noses, thereby creating much dissonance and emotional pain for themselves and each other.

The social therapeutic approach deconstructs and reorganizes that dissonance-making activity; that is, we take it apart and put it back together again by creating an environment in which the representationalist-functionalist bias doesn't overdetermine what people can do.

What can Patti, Mom and Dad do together? All kinds of things — they can dance together. They can write a poem together. They can bake a pie together. And they can create their own language together. *Very nice,* you may be thinking. *But what about the fact that they really do have different positions?* Well, what about it? That's life. If these three people can't do anything together, how — short of outright physical coercion — can Mom and Dad affect Patti? A model of language which insists that everyone must have the same opinion may work out okay for talking about the stars. But it's a disaster when we're talking about people and our infinitely varied views.

The alternative to being locked into a set of judgments — "my position" — is to create an environment together in which everyone has the opportunity to choose a new way of speaking, where ever-changing differences are supported, and where uniformity and conformity are not required presuppositions. You can create such an environment in the practical activities of everyday life. It actually works much better for everyone.

Why? Because in order to help people deal effectively with their humiliation and mortification and shame, it's necessary to create a new, non-representationalist, non-functionalist model of language: a language that's rooted in the activity of creating language. In social therapy we are teaching people like Al and Diane, Mom, Dad and Patti, Donna, Mike and Mike's parents how to build environments where it's possible to engage societal assumptions continuously and, in doing so, to create new languages, new emotions and a new emotionality.

EXERCISE:

This may help you to take a step away from ordinary conversation so you can take a look at language as an activity.

Spend an hour talking without ever saying anything *about* anything else.

28

Development Takes Practice: That's Our Theory

The theory of the social therapeutic approach has grown, and continues to grow, out of our practice, rather than the other way around. Indeed, theory and practice are, for us, an indivisible unity with practice leading the way.

It's important to point this out in light of the traditional and "official" view of science, which is that theory is and ought to be a thing in itself — separate and apart from practice or method. That view, along with the concepts that are fundamental to it — including causality, truth, identity, the subject/self/"I"/consciousness — has in the past quarter of a century or so been subjected to a rigorous critique.

A whole bunch of thinkers have devoted considerable energy to demystifying and "deconstructing" science: postmodern, "poststructuralist" thinkers like Jacques Derrida, Michel Foucault, Kenneth Gergen, Jurgen Habermas, Richard Rorty, John Shotter and many others, as well as feminist philosophers like Sandra Harding, Merill B. Hintikka, Allison Jagger, Nancy Tuana and many others.

Among other things, the idealized notion of the scientific method has come under their critical microscope. In an essay called "Method, Social Science, and Social Hope," the American philosopher Richard Rorty points out that working scientists "use the same banal and obvious methods all of us use in every human activity. They check off examples against criteria; they fudge the counter-examples enough to avoid the need for new models; they try out various guesses, formulated within the current jargon, in the hope of coming up with something which will cover the unfudgeable cases."

With all due respect to the high school teachers, college professors, Hollywood movie makers and journalists who portray scientific activity idealistically, the so-called "hard" sciences — astronomy, biology, chemistry, physics and the rest — are in fact not guided by Theoretical Thinking (capital T and capital T) which supposedly leads in a straight line to Ideas (capital I) that in turn generate the great Discoveries (capital D), Explanations (capital E) and Inventions (capital I). Rather, they're guided by the same kind of thinking that ordinary people do in everyday life: scientists try things out, they advance by trial and error, they do things not knowing what they're doing (which sometimes turn out to be useful), they get ideas (in the shower or while they're doing the dishes) that may or may not come to anything... The point is that practical research science is far less linear, less deductive, less cerebral, a far less "knowing" and vastly more emergent activity than is usually acknowledged.

Not just the method, but the structure of scientific thought itself, has been the object of some serious "the emperor has no clothes" scrutinizing. One of the sharpest scrutinizers was Ludwig Wittgenstein, the eccentric Viennese-born genius who's regarded by many people as the greatest philosopher of the 20th century — in a play I wrote called *Outing Wittgenstein,* his alter-ego describes him as "a Class A European smarty-pants." Nearly half a century ago Wittgenstein got a methodological jump on the deconstructionists when he asked: What if there are no explanations at all?

Wittgenstein, whose early training was in aeronautical engineering, wasn't questioning the content of particular explanations in philosophy, psychology or anything else; he was challenging the methodological assumptions and constructs that together make up the foundation of Western thought — the deadening presuppositions which prevent us from seeing the world clearly. One such assumption is that everything — or anything! — must have an explanation.

Now, no one denies that these "structures of science" have been useful. I don't think there can be any serious doubt that, over the last 200 years, Western science and technology have produced some extraordinary discoveries, all of them significant and many of them enormously beneficial for billions of people throughout the world. (To be sure, many others have been dreadfully misused.) However, it does not follow from this remarkable achievement that science thus constructed applies to the study of human life as lived. Nor is there any reason why it should.

As I have pointed out in earlier chapters, we humans are quite different from everything else in the world which science studies in that only we have the capacity for continuous qualitative transformation. In other words, only we create science. That uniquely emergent, self-reflexive characteristic of our species, which is that we ourselves are among the things we study, requires, it seems to me, a science of development. I'm not talking about a science that has a "branch" devoted to development, or a science that regards development as a "stage" in human life, or a science that views development as an aberration or an abnormality, but a science that takes development as both its object and subject of study. Such a science must be itself developmental and emergent. It must study itself even as it studies everything else. It must be not quantitative but qualitative in its sensibility. It must not be governed by "rules" or "laws"; rather, its rules and tools must come continuously out of its practice.

The social therapeutic approach has been greatly influenced by the work of Lev Vygotsky, the early Soviet psychologist my colleague Lois Holzman and I wrote about in our book *Lev Vygotsky: Revolutionary Scientist*. Dr. Holzman, an internationally prominent developmental psychologist, is the director of an independent laboratory school in New York City for grades K through 8, the Barbara Taylor School, where a Vygotskian approach to education, influenced by social therapy, is both practiced and advanced.

Vygotsky's observations about how very young children learn language led him to believe that the "natural" environment in which children learn is one where learning and development are a unity in which learning leads development — that is, an environment where children are supported to do what they don't know how to do. Although Vygotsky called this kind of environment a "zone of proximal development," he was referring not to a place but to a "joint activity" which "inexperienced speakers" (very young children) and "experienced speakers" (adults and older children) create together.

If it weren't the case that young children participate in a zpd, there would be no accounting for the extraordinary developmental leaps — including the all-important acquisition of language — that human beings make in the first few years of life. Much more importantly — that is, in real life — there couldn't be such qualitative transformation without what Vygotsky called "the only learning worthy of the name": learning that "leads" (is in advance of and includes) development.

That this is the actual process through which human beings develop is often ignored or denied in conventional thinking about thinking. The prevailing "wisdom" insists that cognition (knowing) is primary — just as science itself "puts out the story" that theory (the Idea) somehow precedes and is superior to practice. Accordingly, traditional psychology as applied in the classroom and the therapy office assumes that human beings have to know the rules and understand the reasons before they can learn or change.

That approach, an expression of psychology's misguided attempt to mold itself in the image of physics, is not only profoundly flawed scientifically; it is also, regardless of the intentions, the philosophy or the wishes of its practitioners, profoundly anti-developmental. Which is why Lev Vygotsky urged, more than 70 years ago, that it is necessary to create our own psychology. This new psychology must be rigorously anti-instrumentalist. It must understand "tools" not as tools for results but as tools and results. As Vygotsky put it, in such a psychology "the method is simultaneously prerequisite and product..."

Over the last two decades I have been working with my colleagues at the East Side Institute for Short Term Psychotherapy and the East Side Center for Social Therapy to create a clinical psychology in the image of the human beings we seek to help — to come up with a way of understanding (an approach to) human life which is first and foremost not coercive and which, after that, can be used as a tool and result to create the conditions for continuously reinitiating development.

It's frequently assumed that the secret of success, at least in the "getting and spending" world of work, is the ability to "think big" — code words for quantitative thinking about how to get more and more of what there is. Paradoxically, "thinking big" starts with the assumption that there's a limited number of things in the world, however big that number may be. Thinking big means figuring out how you, your department, and your company can accumulate as many of them as you can. As such, it's an essentially societal — individualistic, acquisitive, competitive, quantitative and particularistic — way of thinking and being.

Now I'm not knocking it — as I've said in earlier chapters, people can learn to be better at getting. Moreover, in a culture of getting it's not an unreasonable thing to want to be. However, I don't think you can assume that getting good at getting necessarily leads to greater gratification, or to development. As I've also said, it's my experience that very successful getters — people who are especially good at thinking big — are as likely to be miserable, dissatisfied and underdeveloped as people who are much less good at getting.

I'm not making a moral or religious point here — I'm not saying that "money doesn't buy happiness" or that "it's harder for a camel to pass through the eye of a needle than it is for a rich man (or woman) to enter Heaven." What I am saying is that the qualities which enable people to adapt, or adjust, most successfully to a culture of getting are frequently irrelevant, and in some cases impediments, to human growth. Thinking big is an example of that. The social therapeutic approach helps people to think totalistically and developmentally, as opposed to big.

If you've already read some of the earlier chapters in this book, no doubt you'll have noticed that I have a lot to say on "particulars" and "totalities." The relationship between them is the subject of a very old philosophical debate which goes back more than 2,000 years, all the way to the Greeks who were philosophizing even before that Plato fellow was a sparkle in his mother's eye.

That's very interesting, you may say (politely). *But so what? What's that got to do with my life, here and now?* Well, from a social therapeutic standpoint, the notion of the particular — that is, the thing, along with its temporal companionpiece, the beginning point — is one of the great fictions of Western culture. So far as I can see, there are no particulars. There are no "things" that can be separated, except by force — especially by force of definition, which is to say non-developmentally — from the seamless historical totality that has no beginning, middle or end, no starting point. In fact, it has no point at all.

Yet the notion of the particular, accompanied by the notion that what we can change and all we can change are particulars — particular Problems, particular Behaviors, particular Individuals — has had an enormous influence on how we see and experience the world, including ourselves and our species as viewed through the particularity-biased, pseudo-scientific lens of Freudian and neo-Freudian psychology. Freud himself, by the way, often expressed his admiration for the scientific worldview.

It is because there are no particulars that it isn't possible to transform them developmentally. That is, a "thing" — a "habit," a "self," a "relationship," a "situation" — can be changed only by wrenching it out of its historical totality and manipulating it. A special ed teacher can modify a student's behavior with rewards and punishments; a surgeon can suck the fat out of someone's thighs; parents can "make" their child practice the piano or clean her room; psychiatrists, like their counterparts on the street, can alter people's moods and behavior with drugs. Does any of this change things? Apparently, yes. Does it lead to development, to growth? There's no evidence that it does.

Now fictions can sometimes entertain us, and some may even be useful — to whom, and for what purpose, are different issues. I would argue strongly that the fiction of the particular, as employed by Western science over the last 300 years to alter nature — from building transcontinental highways to curing contagious diseases — has been highly useful to hundreds of billions of people. And I would argue just as strongly that the notion of the particular, which is increasingly associated with coercion in contemporary societal life, has outlived its usefulness and come to stand in the way of further human development.

All societies, not just Western society, tend to turn their particular "truths" into universals — to transpose the particulars of this time and this place to the realm of the universal, where how "we" are and what "we" do become identified as the human norm. This tension between society and history, the elevation of particular features of a society to the abstract level of universal truth, makes it very difficult, and sometimes impossible, not only for people to see historically, but even to know that there is anything other than their own society. When society dominates to such a degree that genuine historical understanding is negated by societal universalization, then no real development can take place.

The social therapeutic approach tries to teach people how to think as creators and transformers of everything that there is and all there is — in other words, as makers of history. From our perspective, history is not the name of some "thing" with spatial or temporal dimensions, a "collection" of innumerable, arbitrarily fragmented, discrete particulars, the sum of its past-present-future parts, but a process: the beginning-less, end-less, endlessly interconnected, human-made totality of totalities, including the world and ourselves in it.

Historical thinking isn't quantitative but qualitative; that is, it asks how rather than how much or how soon. It does not compel the thinker to adopt the mythic identity of an isolated, individuated "self" in competition with other selves, but reaffirms the individual's actual connection to every other human being as a member of the human species. The historical statement is not the "I think, therefore I am" of Rene Descartes, but "We create, therefore we are."

What is it to be a human being? Albert Einstein, a great humanist as well as a great scientist, believed that it is not possible to exclude the measurer from the measurement. The notion that the measurer, the thinker, the human being, can be objectified as if he or she were no different from the thing measured (the object thought), Einstein said, is nonsensical. Historical thinking engages the relationship between — the totality of — the individual thinker and the thought he or she is thinking, which are inextricably connected. This is what we mean by historical subjectivity. It is this totality that is important, from a social therapeutic point of view.

What's most significant about social therapy is that it's not simply a humanistic critique of the myth of psychology and the role it plays in providing a pseudo-scientific rationale for coercion. The social therapeutic approach is a practice; it is a practical, noncoercive response to the challenge first posed by Lev Vygotsky in the early part of this century, which was reframed by Ludwig Wittgenstein some 30 years later, and stated again in this postmodern moment by the deconstructionists and their colleagues the critical theorists — a challenge to reconstruct an epistemology, a way of knowing, which is usable for learning new ways of developing at a moment when human development in many areas of life has come to a standstill.

The social therapeutic approach locates human freedom not in the societally determined "right" to change particular behaviors, but in our species' unlimited capacity to engage in the historical activity of continuously transforming totalities. It is not about "self-discovery" — it is people, all people, making history together in the infinitude of activities that make up human existence.

EXERCISE:

Here's something to help you see the relationship between theory and practice.

The next time someone says something theoretical to you, ask her or him: "Okay. What's the practical value of all that?"

About the authors

Fred Newman is the creator of social therapy, a clinical approach that uses performance rather than psychology to cure people of their emotional problems and psychopathology. A practicing therapist in New York City for nearly 30 years, Dr. Newman is the founder and the director of training at the East Side Institute for Short Term Psychotherapy, which offers certificate programs and short courses in the social therapeutic approach. In addition to the East Side Center for Social Therapy, located in Manhattan, there are social therapy centers in Atlanta, Boston, Philadelphia, San Francisco, Saratoga (NY), and Washington, D.C.

Dr. Newman has lectured extensively throughout the United States and abroad, and periodically conducts performance training workshops in New York and other cities. He is the creator of Performance of a Lifetime, a school for performance in everyday life, and is the host of a radio call-in show, "Let's Develop!," which is heard throughout the New York metropolitan area every Sunday at noon on WEVD-AM 1050. A playwright and theatre director, Dr. Newman is the artistic director of the off-off-Broadway Castillo Theatre in New York City, a showcase for his developmental theatre.

Dr. Newman received his doctorate in the philosophy of science from Stanford University. He is the author of several books including *Performance of a Lifetime: A Practical Philosophical Guide to the Joyous Life* (with Phyllis Goldberg) and is the co-author with Lois Holzman of *Lev Vygotsky: Revolutionary Scientist*, *Unscientific Psychology: A Cultural Performatory Approach to Understanding Human Life* and *The End of Knowing: A New Developmental Way of Learning*. A longtime political activist, Dr. Newman has played a leading role in efforts to build a national third party in the United States.

Phyllis Goldberg is an educator who holds a doctorate in sociology from New York University. Over the last 20 years she has collaborated with Dr. Newman on a variety of writing projects, including his book *Performance of a Lifetime*. Dr. Goldberg is currently working on a biography of Fred Newman.

Index

abnormal psychology. *See* psychology
abuse, 13-14, 81
Abusive Behavior Syndrome, 14
activity, 24, 64-65, 82, 103, 157, 184
addiction: to alcohol and/or drugs,
    22, 91-97; to food, 150; the myth
    of, 91-95, 98; and social control,
    93; 12-step programs, 91, 95, 97,
    179
aging, 47-49, 107, 125
aggression, 67, 70-72
AIDS, 161
alcoholism. *See* addiction
alienation, 212
anger: and chronic illness, 105
anxiety, 159-160
appearance: and choice, 147-149;
    competition, 145; and exploita-
    tion, 147-148; and the getting
    game, 146, 148; and humiliation,
    149; and women's subjugation,
    145-146
assertiveness, 201-204
attention deficit disorder, 92
attraction. *See* sexual attraction

Barbara Taylor School, 232
Bateson, Gregory, 220
behavior: and abuse, 14; going
    through the motions, 11-13; mod-
    ification, 14-15; and roles, 13

behaviorism, 14
biological determinism, 124, 155
blame, 98, 106
brainwashing, 14
breaking up, 127-136

change. *See* transformation
child rearing. *See* parenting
children: and completing, 63, 65;
    drug treatment for, 157; labeling
    of, 153-154; and play, 122-124;
    radical acceptance of, 58; building
    relationships with, 58; worldly-
    wise, 51-53
choice (*see also* decision-making): ver-
    sus addiction model, 93-98; and
    appearance, 147-149; child rearing
    strategies, 149, 199-200; and
    chronic illness, 108; and the
    capacity to develop, 13, 98, 156;
    drug treatment and denial of, 98,
    156; of how to live, 12, 108, 123-
    124, 149; and performing roles,
    123
chronic illness (*see also* pain), 104-108
coercion, 14, 48, 235
communication, 38-40
communicationalists, 219-224
competition: and appearance, 145;
    and assertiveness, 201; versus com-
    pletion, 62-64; and a culture of

More from Dr. Fred Newman

Performance of a Lifetime
A Practical-Philosophical Guide to the Joyous Life
by Fred Newman with Phyllis Goldberg
In the sequel to *Let's Develop!*, this iconoclastic philosopher shows readers how to live joyously by asking philosophical questions about our everyday lives. *244 pages $11.95 (Castillo International)*

The Myth of Psychology
by Fred Newman
A fascinating and provocative book that explodes the myths on which psychology is based! Topics include addiction, depression, panic and transference. *229 pages $12.95 (Castillo International)*

Still on the Corner and Other Postmodern Political Plays by Fred Newman
Edited by Dan Friedman
Fred Newman sees his plays as experiments in developmental activity. This collection of 19 of these performatory experiments, reflecting his first decade as a playwright, marks Newman's emergence as an original and controversial voice in the theatre.
700 pages $24.95 (Castillo Cultural Center)

The End of Knowing A New Developmental Way of Learning
by Fred Newman and Lois Holzman
What if knowing — long thought to be the key to human progress — has now become an impediment to further human development? This book addresses the practical question of how to reconstruct our world when modernist ideas have failed to solve many social problems.
240 pages $19.95 (Routledge)

Community Literacy Research Project, Inc.
500 Greenwich Street, Suite 201, New York, NY 10013

Phone: 212-941-9400 Fax: 212-941-8340 Order online: www.castillo.org